# Spirit-filled Discipleship

How God Calls Christlike Disciples

David Fleming

Disciples Ignited

Copyright © 2022 by David B Fleming

All rights reserved.

No portion of this book may be reproduced in any form without written permission from the publisher or author, except as permitted by U.S. copyright law.

ISBN: 978-0-9723048-2-5

SPIRIT-FILLED DISCIPLESHIP: HOW GOD CALLS CHRISTLIKE DISCIPLES is the first book of the SPIRIT-FILLED DISCIPLESHIP SERIES.

SPIRIT-FILLED DISCIPLESHIP: HOW GOD CALLS CHRISTLIKE DISCIPLES is a revised and updated version of section one of DISCIPLESHIP FOR A NEW GENERATION, published by the same author in 2000.

Scripture quotations marked NIV are taken from THE HOLY BIBLE, NEW INTERNATIONAL VERSION®, copyright © 1973, 1978, 1984, 2011 by Biblica, Inc.™ Used by permission. All rights reserved worldwide.

Scripture quotations marked ESV are taken from the ESV® Bible (The Holy Bible, English Standard Version®), copyright © 2001 by Crossway Bibles, a publishing ministry of Good News Publishers. Used by permission. All rights reserved.

This book is dedicated to my daughter,

Casey Fleming Copeland

who has been called by Jesus to labor in what I believe will be the greatest harvest the Church has ever seen!

# Special Thanks

I am forever grateful to the Lord Jesus for His love and the help He has given me through so many people who have all played a part in helping me author this book.

To my wife, Carol, who has lovingly stood by my side since 1975. I am deeply indebted and thankful for her wholehearted love for Jesus, her powerful prayers, and her faithful service in the Kingdom of God. I am blessed that we are joined together in life and ministry.

To my parents, Mr. & Mrs. B.R. Fleming, who brought me up in the ways of the Lord. I am forever thankful to the Lord that He blessed me with such godly and wise parents.

To Apostle Joel Laurore who is responsible for the birthing and impartation of the truths I have sought to write about in this book.

To Dr. Roxanne Mitchell for her helpful comments and editorial assistance.

# Preface

You may have just begun the glorious journey of becoming a disciple of Jesus Christ, or you may have been following the Lord for quite some time. Whichever is the case, I believe that you will gain much as you study the principles of discipleship presented in this series titled SPIRIT-FILLED DISCIPLESHIP. The series was written to help you gain insight into how God calls, prepares, and reveals Christlike disciples.

Unfortunately, as far as ministry is concerned, many in the Church make a big distinction between the ministers of the Church and the congregation. Such a mindset delegates all ministry to those who hold leadership positions in the Church. However, that wasn't the belief nor practice of the New Testament Church. When the Church first began all the disciples of Jesus ministered, in the Church and throughout the world they lived in!

**The fact that God has called all disciples of Jesus to represent the life and ministry of Jesus is foundational to understanding true Biblical discipleship and is the approach taken in these books.**

I originally published this book in 2000 under the title DISCIPLESHIP FOR A NEW GENERATION but I am now offering it as a series made up of three books.

- SPIRIT-FILLED DISCIPLESHIP: HOW GOD CALLS CHRISTLIKE DISCIPLES
- SPIRIT-FILLED DISCIPLESHIP: HOW GOD PREPARES CHRISTLIKE DISCIPLES
- SPIRIT-FILLED DISCIPLESHIP: HOW GOD REVEALS CHRISTLIKE DISCIPLES

The entire subject matter of the previously published book, DISCIPLESHIP FOR A NEW GENERATION, is contained in these three books but the content has been thoroughly revised and updated. I have also included questions throughout each chapter where I encourage you to *Pause & Reflect* on that which you just read.

Each book of this series will stand on its own. However, the series is meant to be read in sequence. I encourage you to read these books devotionally. Embrace the truths that are presented in each segment and ponder them until they permeate your heart and mind. Use the *Pause & Reflect* portion of each section to help you. I believe that if you answer the questions after each segment in a thorough, honest manner that you will be encouraged, challenged, and ignited to serve Jesus as did the early followers of Jesus who changed the world!

God bless you as you proceed.

Dr. David B. Fleming

# Foreword

No age, in the history of our planet, has seen such high degree of deception with men and women presenting themselves as true disciples of Jesus Christ.

No one has the right to talk or write about discipleship except the man who himself is an engaged true disciple of Jesus Christ. Dr. David Fleming's life and deeds have been eloquently testifying that, against so many odds of time and space. The right to discuss this so important subject, in a literary manner, is his legitimate privilege. And the Holy Spirit unction rests upon him, awakening the dead in his prophetic utterances, in precision, arresting the attention of hearers. All that would make this book so alive to serious lovers and seekers of Jesus Christ.

These pages are pregnant with Biblical truths, with revelations and with the rich experience of many years of walking with Jesus, following Him, often in most difficult times.

This is far from being just a "nice thing" to read, it is a Heaven-approved presentation and a compelling exhortation to follow in all truth, in all sincerity, Him Who is the Way, the Truth, the Life.

The body of Christ in the state of Florida has been holding a precious secret: the Jesus filled ministry of this author, released into all directions. It will certainly be followed by a great Holy Spirit outpouring, a wonderful revival move; that is the secret historical order, that is the Biblical pattern, that is the Jesus holy prescription.

The Lord Jesus, in our day, is calling and raising true Spirit-filled disciples, because they are carriers of Jesus Christ and His Holy Spirit, God's blueprint for world salvation, in their apostolic proclamation of the Name above all names, the Only Hope of a world plunged into despair without Jesus, as Prophet Fleming is so strikingly sharing.

Read this book, but read it hunger filled, read it profitably, read it Jesus seeking, and your rewarding portion will be beyond description.

Apostle Joseph Joel Laurore
World Revival Temple, Tulsa, OK

# Endorsement

This book is very critical and timely as we take a serious look at the Christian church today. As we have seen the growth and spread of the Gospel over the past two centuries, it has come largely as a result of Spirit-filled followers of Christ. Jesus called many to be disciples and after training them, He told them to stay in Jerusalem until they received the Holy Spirit. He knew that they would not be able to carry out the work without the Holy Spirit. (Acts 1:4-8)

This book is a must read for every person who is called to be a follower of Christ, and to fulfill that calling. Our culture has shifted so drastically in recent years that it is imperative that we prepare to meet the challenges we are facing. There is so much emphasis on deconstruction of beliefs, loss of absolute truth, false cults and attacks on Christian faith. I strongly recommend this book for every pastor, teacher, leader, and Christ follower. I also commend Dr. David Fleming for producing such a deep work on the need for Spirit-filled disciples.

Bishop Billy Baskin
Pastor emeritus, New Way Fellowship Praise and Worship Church, Miami Gardens, FL

# Contents

1. Called To Be Disciples　　　　　　　　　　　　　　　1
   Elisha Was Called To Be A Disciple
   Recognizing God-Appointed Leadership
   Disciples Are Called To Serve
   Disciples Don't Need To Be Begged
   Disciples Anointed With The Spirit
   Disciples Who Become True Sons
   Disciples Of The Double Portion
   Disciples Who Grow In The Anointing Of Their Leaders
   Disciples Who Forsake All For The Sake Of The Call

2. Called To Be Ministers Of The Old & New Wine　　　37
   Satisfied With The Familiar?
   "Old Wine" And "New Wine"
   Your Attitude Towards "Old Wine"
   The Power Released In "New Wine"
   The "Old" And "New" Working Together

3. Called To Demonstrate The Gospel Of Jesus Christ　54
   Elisha Desired To Demonstrate God's Power
   It Takes The Cross To Demonstrate The Gospel
   Receiving Impartation From Your Leadership
   Demonstrating The Gospel Reveals Jesus Christ

Picking Up The Mantle

# Chapter One

# Called To Be Disciples

The prayers of Christ and the Church for worldwide revival are being answered in fulfillment of Joel 2:28-29.

> *And afterward, I will pour out my Spirit on all people. Your sons and daughters will prophesy, your old men will dream dreams, your young men will see visions. Even on my servants, both men and women, I will pour out my Spirit in those days. (Joel 2:28-29, NIV)*

This promised outpouring is bringing about the greatest revelation of Jesus Christ the world has ever known. Yet, there is much more ahead! The revelation of Jesus that is now being experienced by so many is going to grow exponentially bringing multitudes to repentance and faith in Him. The Kingdom of God is going to increase immeasurably in dramatic and miraculous ways!

During this end time revival, I believe that we are going to see the literal fulfillment of the prophecy of Jesus recorded in John 14:12.

> *Very truly I tell you, whoever believes in me will do the works I have been doing, and they will do even greater things than these, because I am going to the Father. (John 14:12, NIV)*

Now, how is such an astounding prophecy going to be fulfilled? There answer is simple. It's going to be fulfilled through sold-out disciples for Jesus! So, whether you have just begun to follow Jesus, or whether you have known Him for years and are now experiencing a fresh outpouring of His Spirit, Jesus is calling you to a deeper level of discipleship where you will become like Him in life and ministry! If you are such a person, this book is written for you.

The Bible is full of examples of those who answered the call of God to become disciples. One such person was Elisha. Since the Biblical pattern concerning the call to discipleship is so easily seen in Elisha's life, his life and ministry will be used as the basis of our study in this section.

## Elisha Was Called To Be A Disciple

There is not a lot written about Elisha before he received his call into the ministry except that he was the son of Shaphat from Abel Meholah, of the tribe of Issachar and that his name in Hebrew means, "God is Salvation." However, the Bible is clear that a dramatic change took place in Elisha the day that Elijah called him to become a disciple. The Lord had plans to use Elisha in powerful ways to reveal the salvation of the Lord, but first he had to answer God's call.

One of the basic lessons that you must learn about being a disciple of the Lord Jesus is that Jesus will use leadership to help form you into a vessel that He can use. The Lord will unite you with the one He has chosen to make you into a useful disciple. An excellent example of this is Elijah who was given the responsibility to prepare Elisha to fulfill his destiny. In fact, Elisha would never have been able to fulfill his calling had he not been willing to be mentored by Elijah. So, in order to understand the call of God upon Elisha's life, you must view it in relationship to his call to follow Elijah the prophet.

It is interesting that God used Elijah to reveal Elisha's call into the ministry. It even appears that God first revealed His plan concerning Elisha to Elijah, and then used Elijah to reveal it to Elisha!

> ... anoint Elisha son of Shaphat from Abel Meholah to succeed you as prophet. (1 Kings 19:16, NIV)

This shows that the Lord may reveal His plan concerning you to a spiritual leader before He does to you. It's really not uncommon for godly leadership to know more about your calling than you do. That, of course, doesn't mean that the Lord isn't going to speak to you personally. However, you must be open to the various ways that the Lord will speak to you. The Lord could have first spoken to Elisha about his calling and then told him to go find Elijah, but instead the Lord did the opposite. Thankfully Elisha was open to the Lord using leadership to give him guidance. At the very least, the calling of Elisha through Elijah should teach disciples to listen to God appointed spiritual elders and allow God to use them in their lives as He desires. The Church needs to understand the importance that Jesus puts on leadership and their influence in the lives of His disciples. As a principle, the Lord does not work alone, but uses those He has already called to be of great influence in the lives of those He is presently calling.

*So Christ himself gave the apostles, the prophets, the evangelists, the pastors and teachers, to equip his people for works of service, so that the body of Christ may be built up (Ephesians 4:11–12, NIV)*

When you look at the spiritual leadership that preceded Elijah, you'll find that Eli was used by the Lord to teach and train Samuel to fulfill his destiny. However, because Eli had major problems involving disobedience to the Lord, his ability to impart into Samuel's life was severely impaired. Eli's influence would have been much greater had he lived what he taught! In contrast, God was able to use Elijah to more fully teach and train Elisha to fulfill his destiny because Elijah followed the Lord wholeheartedly in righteousness and holiness.

The need for godly leadership and submission to it is easily seen by looking at Church history. The Jesus Movement of the 1960's and 1970's reveals the need for submission to godly leadership. During that sovereign move of God the Lord poured out His Spirit on an entire generation of young people in America. However, some young people weren't as open to godly leadership as they should have been. Granted, there were many in leadership who were threatened by the work that God was doing in and through the young people, but there were also leaders who embraced it with great joy. Sad to say, many of the young people who disregarded godly leadership fell away. They lacked the spiritual protection that leadership would have given them during the tests, trials, temptations, and persecution that came their way. Thankfully, those who submitted to godly leadership were better able to stand when the enemy sought their destruction.

Unfortunately, it is often a temptation for a younger generation to look at the mistakes and shortcomings of their elders and thus disregard what they have to say. Elisha certainly could have looked at Elijah and found mistakes and shortcomings. Hadn't

Elijah fallen into a deep depression right after being used by God to destroy the prophets of Baal on Mt. Carmel?[1] The point is this, the leadership that God uses to call and train you won't be perfect in every way. Yet, God will use them in your life to help prepare you and impart into you that which you'll need to fulfill your calling!

Therefore, as a disciple of the Lord Jesus you should anticipate that the Lord will unite you with Christlike leadership. The role that godly leadership will have in making you into a disciple is very significant. There are a few exceptions in Church history where God raised up men and women to Church leadership that had no mentor. However, God's principal means of preparing His disciples has always been through Christlike leadership.

### *Pause & Reflect*

1. Elisha's name means, "God is salvation." In the Old Testament period people were often given names that revealed their character and destiny. What do you think Elisha's name tells us about his destiny?

2. What part did Elijah the prophet have in helping Elisha fulfill his destiny?

3. Can you think of any other mentors in the Bible? Make a list of their name(s) and at least one of their disciples.

4. Moses was a leader of the Israelites, but he was specifically a mentor to Joshua. (Exodus 33:11) The Apostle Paul won many converts to Jesus, but he had a special mentoring relationship with Timothy whom he called his "son in the faith" (1 Timothy 1:2, NIV). In a mentoring relationship why can't your mentor be your "buddy?"

5. What did Elijah know about Elisha that Elisha may not have known about himself? (1 Kings 19:16b)

6. Elijah was told by God that Elisha would succeed him as prophet. However, Elijah didn't tell Elisha that when he called him to be his disciple. Why was Elijah wise in NOT sharing that revelation with Elisha, at least not at the beginning of their mentoring relationship?

## Recognizing God-Appointed Leadership

How will you be able to recognize the person that God has appointed to be your leader? How did Elisha know that he should follow Elijah? First of all, the person that God appoints to be a mentor in your life will be godly. But how can you tell if someone is godly? Jesus spoke on this very issue when He said,

> Watch out for false prophets. They come to you in sheep's clothing, but inwardly they are ferocious wolves. By their fruit you will recognize them. Do people pick grapes from thornbushes, or figs from thistles? Likewise, every good tree bears good fruit, but a bad tree bears bad fruit. A good tree cannot bear bad fruit, and a bad tree cannot bear good fruit. (Matthew 7:15–18, NIV)

Just as a grape vine reveals its fruit through its branches the Lord Jesus reveals the fruit of the Spirit through His disciples.

> But the fruit of the Spirit is love, joy, peace, patience, kindness, goodness, faithfulness, gentleness, self-control; (Galatians 5:22–23, ESV)

The fruit of the Spirit reveals that a person is abiding in Jesus.[2] It speaks of a certain amount of spiritual maturity. It reveals godly character. That's why the fruit of the Spirit is absolutely necessary for every leader! Just because a person has natural charisma and is able to attract a large following doesn't mean that he or she is a godly leader. Godly leadership is based on godly character (fruit) not charisma. Unfortunately, there are ungodly people with natural charisma who attract large followings. Yet, the path that they would lead you on wouldn't be conducive to a Christlike life and ministry. It takes a leader with the fruit of the Spirit to be able to nurture Christlikeness in others.

We must also reckon with the fact that some people are drawn to follow leaders solely on the basis of their miraculous ministry. Miraculous ministry is very important, but you can't judge someone's godliness by the spiritual gifts that are operative in his or her life.

> Now to each one the manifestation of the Spirit is given for the common good. To one there is given through the Spirit a message of wisdom, to another a message of knowledge by means of the same Spirit, to another faith by the same Spirit, to another gifts of healing by that one Spirit, to another miraculous powers, to another prophecy, to another distinguishing between spirits, to another speaking in different kinds of tongues, and to still another the interpretation of tongues. All these are the work of one and the same Spirit, and he distributes them to each one, just as he determines. (1 Corinthians 12:7-11, NIV)

Spiritual gifts are necessary in the lives of all spiritual leaders. However, the gifts of the Holy Spirit (which make a ministry miraculous) must be seen for what they are. They are gifts, freely given by God to all Christians who desire them and will receive them by faith. Even Christians who have just been "born again" can receive miraculous ministry gifts from the Holy Spirit.

Therefore, spiritual gifts mustn't be viewed as a sign of spiritual maturity. For example, Elijah was used by God in miraculous ways. Yet, Elijah's miraculous ministry didn't prove that he was spiritually mature. His spiritual maturity was proved by the fact that he was a godly man!

Of course, the ultimate example of godly leadership is seen in the Lord Jesus Himself! He is the epitome of godliness and the miraculous. Thankfully, the Lord has leadership that is following in His footsteps. They are revealing Jesus in their lives (through the fruit of the Spirit) as well as their ministries (through the gifts of the Spirit). They will help prepare you to fulfill your destiny. I pray that when the Lord brings them into your life that you will have the perception to recognize them and follow their leadership!

### *Pause & Reflect*

1. How will you be able to recognize the person that God has appointed to be your leader? (Matthew 7:17-18)

2. In Matthew 7:16 Jesus used fruit as a metaphor of godly character. What character traits (fruits) are necessary for godly leaders to manifest? (Galatians 5:22-23)

3. A gift is that which is freely given whereas fruit comes from a seed which requires a process of growth. What does this reveal concerning the gifts of the Spirit mentioned in 1 Corinthians 12:7-11 and the fruits of the Spirit mentioned in Galatians 5:22-23?

4. Why do you think that Godly leadership requires godly character?

5. How do the fruits of the Spirit compliment the gifts of Spirit in the life of a Christian?

6. What are you looking for in a mentor?

## Disciples Are Called To Serve

It is important to notice that the Lord didn't initially speak to Elisha about his own ministry but about following Elijah. In other words, God first called Elisha to help another person in his ministry! I'm sure that the Lord did that for many reasons, but one beneficial result was that it gave Elisha an opportunity to develop a humble servant's heart. As Jesus taught: "The greatest among you will be your servant. For those who exalt themselves will be humbled, and those who humble themselves will be exalted." (Matthew 23:11-12, NIV)

So, even though Elisha was going to have one of the greatest ministries of the Old Testament prophets, he was first called by the Lord to be a servant to Elijah. The Lord uses this same means of calling people today. A call to greatness is a call to servitude! If you are to fulfill God's purpose for your life you must be willing to become a servant. That's exactly what Elisha had to do. God's plan for Elisha was to be a prophet, but first he had to be Elijah's servant.

> *Then he set out to follow Elijah and became his servant. (1 Kings 19:21, NIV)*

The Hebrew word used here for "servant" is not the same one used to describe the work of a slave. It more closely describes the ministry of an assistant or an aide. Just as Joshua was called to aid Moses, Elisha was called to aid Elijah.

> *Then Moses set out with Joshua his aide, and Moses went up on the mountain of God. (Exodus 24:13, NIV)*

But whether you call it being a servant or being an aide, the ministry is the same: humble service as was seen in the life and ministry of the Lord Jesus. Speaking of the humble servitude of Jesus, Paul wrote,

> ... he made himself nothing by taking the very nature of a servant, being made in human likeness. (Philippians 2:7, NIV)

Scripture clearly shows that leadership is never given the authority of a dictator. A dictator is one who uses his power to enforce his own will. True godly leaders never use their authority to enforce their own will, they seek only to enforce the will of the Lord Jesus Christ. That is the type of leadership that the Lord wants to join you to, so that by learning how to submit to and serve Christlike leadership you will learn how to better serve the Lord Jesus.

There have been cases in which those who have been called by God immediately went and started their own ministries. Unfortunately, this has too often led to failure. It's not that they don't have the calling to be a leader. It's just that they haven't been fully prepared through faithful service to God appointed leadership. That's why, although God planned to give Elisha a powerful prophetic ministry, He would not bring it to pass until Elisha learned how to be a servant!

That leads to this truth. The fulfillment of your ministry is often connected to your willingness to assist another in the fulfillment of his or her ministry. This principle I have seen from my own experience. When I first submitted to my leader, I did so fearfully. I was afraid that everything the Lord had shown me about my calling and ministry was somehow going to be lost or swallowed up by the ministry I was being called to submit to. I didn't realize it then, but the vision the Lord had previously revealed to me was but a small part of the ministry He had planned for my life. The Lord had much more to show me! I began to realize that the calling of God on my life would be fulfilled as I submitted myself to the leadership the Lord was calling me to serve. It was when I answered God's call to be a servant and help my leader fulfill his vision that the Lord started fulfilling the promises of ministry He had previously given to me.

This is not to suggest that the Lord won't eventually lead someone to start his or her own ministry. Elisha was given his own ministry after he learned the lessons of servitude. However, I don't believe that Elisha was consumed with the desire to have his own ministry. I believe that Elisha considered it a privilege to serve Elijah, and that the lessons he learned in doing so stayed with him for the rest of his life and helped make him the effective minister that he became.

### *Pause & Reflect*

1. The Lord told Elijah to anoint Elisha as the next prophet but when Elisha first started following Elijah it was more in the role of a servant than a minister (1 Kings 19:16, 21). How did this help prepare Elisha to succeed Elijah as prophet many years later?

2. The fulfillment of your ministry is often connected to your willingness to assist your mentor in the fulfillment of his or her ministry. This requires that you have at least a basic understanding of what God has called your mentor to accomplish. Briefly describe what you have observed and learned about your mentor's ministry.

3. A call to greatness is a call to servitude. How are you serving your God-given mentor? If your mentor has given you specific responsibilities make a list of them. If you have not been given specific responsibilities what do you

believe you can do to help your mentor fulfill his or her destiny?

## Disciples Don't Need To Be Begged

Even though Elijah had received specific revelation concerning Elisha, he didn't beg Elisha to follow him!

> *So Elijah went from there and found Elisha son of Shaphat. He was plowing with twelve yoke of oxen, and he himself was driving the twelfth pair. Elijah went up to him and threw his cloak around him. Elisha then left his oxen and ran after Elijah. "Let me kiss my father and mother goodbye," he said, "and then I will come with you." "Go back," Elijah replied. "What have I done to you?" So Elisha left him and went back. He took his yoke of oxen and slaughtered them. He burned the plowing equipment to cook the meat and gave it to the people, and they ate. Then he set out to follow Elijah and became his servant. (1 Kings 19:19–21, NIV)*

At first it may seem strange that Elijah didn't try to persuade Elisha to follow him after Elisha seemed reluctant, especially since the Lord sent Elijah to anoint Elisha as the next prophet! Yet, Elijah understood that those who have to be begged will never make good disciples! The same approach is seen when Jesus called His disciples. Jesus was very straightforward towards those He called and those who wanted to follow Him. He never tried to hide the absolute surrender that would be required of His disciples.

> *Then a teacher of the law came to him and said, "Teacher, I will follow you wherever you go." Jesus*

> replied, "Foxes have dens and birds have nests, but the Son of Man has no place to lay his head." Another disciple said to him, "Lord, first let me go and bury my father." But Jesus told him, "Follow me, and let the dead bury their own dead. (Matthew 8:19–22, NIV)
>
> In the same way, those of you who do not give up everything you have cannot be my disciples. (Luke 14:33, NIV)

In essence, Jesus told His would-be disciples to "count the cost" before they made any commitment.[3] In retrospect, Elisha was at the threshold of a new beginning of his life and was being called on to leave everything behind. Couldn't he serve both Elijah and his own interests? No, and neither can you. When you answer God's call it must be with an absolute surrender and not a halfhearted, "if everything goes well, I guess so" mentality. Those who realize what an awesome privilege it is to be chosen by God to follow Him are eager and willing to do so. Yet, it should also be a very sobering decision, made with the awareness that Jesus expects your all, or nothing. Thankfully, Elisha realized the opportunity being given him and forsook all to take it!

> He took his yoke of oxen and slaughtered them. He burned the plowing equipment to cook the meat and gave it to the people, and they ate. Then he set out to follow Elijah and became his servant. (1 Kings 19:21, NIV)

Elisha's seriousness in following God's call on his life was seen in the way that he burned the plowing equipment he had been using when Elijah called him to be his disciple. Elisha even celebrated God's call on his life by cooking the very oxen he'd previously used to make a living! When Jesus called his disciples, they had the same type of willingness to give up everything for the Lord.

> Come, follow me," Jesus said, "and I will send you out to fish for people." At once they left their nets and followed him. (Matthew 4:19–20, NIV)

Jesus never begs people to be His disciples. Instead, He calls people to Himself and invites them to follow and start enjoying the abundant life that only He can give. However, make no mistake, to be a disciple of Jesus requires that you give Him your life, withholding nothing. Elisha had to give up his farming, the disciples had to give up their fishing, and you may have to give up that which is dear to you. Yet, that which you will gain from following Jesus will far exceed anything He may require you to give up. Jesus is still calling out, "follow me". Heed His voice and seize your opportunity!

### *Pause & Reflect*

1. What did Elisha do that revealed he was serious about becoming Elijah's devoted disciple? (1 Kings 19:21)

2. What did Jesus mean when He told His would-be disciples to fully contemplate the cost of following Him before they committed themselves to being His disciples? (Luke 14:27-30)

3. Jesus would not allow anyone to follow Him closely unless they were willing to put Him above everything else. (Luke 14:33) Are you putting Jesus above everything else or are you still allowing something (or someone) to hold you back? (Be specific.)

4. What did the disciples of Jesus do that revealed they were serious about following Him? (Matthew 4:19-20)

5. Have you embraced your time of being mentored with the same dedication and seriousness that Jesus requires of His disciples? Such dedication is much more than words, it is seen in your actions. What have you done that reveals your total dedication?

## Disciples Anointed With The Spirit

In the Old Testament the most common way the Lord would show that someone was being anointed for a particular calling was to have the prophet of the Lord pour oil on their head. This method was used by Samuel the prophet when he was sent by the Lord to call and anoint David as the next king of Israel after Saul.

> *So Samuel took the horn of oil and anointed him in the presence of his brothers, and from that day on the Spirit of the Lord came powerfully upon David. (1 Samuel 16:13, NIV)*

However, there's no mention in Scripture of Elijah anointing Elisha with oil. Instead, Elisha was anointed by way of Elijah's cloak.

> *Elijah went up to him and threw his cloak around him. (1 Kings 19.19, NIV)*

The cloak that Elijah threw around Elisha was his outer garment. This common outer garment was usually made of two pieces of thick woolen material or fur sewn together, with slits rather than sleeves for the arms. The typical Hebrew used his cloak as a covering to keep him warm when sleeping. Since this was especially true for travelers, shepherds, or poor people, a person's mantle was not to be kept as collateral for a loan.[4] Thus, the cloak was a very important, but common article used by Jewish males of that day. However, the real significance lies in the cloak's spiritual symbolism. The Hebrew word for cloak (*'addereth'*) not only means 'cloak', but also figuratively signifies 'glory, splendor, and magnificence'.[5] The cloak Elijah put on Elisha signified the power and glory of the Lord's anointing, thus showing that the Lord uses common, lowly people and ordinary things through which He reveals His glory![6] The throwing of Elijah's cloak around Elisha was a unique way the Lord had of imparting the anointing of the Holy Spirit on Elisha, which he would need as he started on the path of preparation to fulfill his calling as a prophet of the Lord.

Why did the Lord do it that way? I'm sure that there are many reasons, one of which is that the Lord is unique and deals with us all according to His will and our needs. But it also taught an important lesson. The anointing Elisha received was united with the person he was being called to follow! From that time on Elijah's cloak symbolized the spiritual covering, protection, and anointing Elisha received by submitting to Elijah.

Another interesting matter is that by throwing his cloak around Elisha, Elijah was signifying the relationship they were to have with one another. Elijah was being called to be a spiritual father to Elisha! In the same way that a father provides, protects, guides, helps, and is an example to his children, so would Elijah be to Elisha. What an awesome responsibility God had given Elijah! He was called to represent the Lord to Elisha and bring him up in the ways of the Lord. He was to be, from that day on, a "spiritual covering" for Elisha. That's why it's so important who your spiritual covering is, for in the same way that Elijah was used to impart a spiritual covering over Elisha, God wants to use the leadership you follow to cover you with the Lord Jesus Christ.

*Rather, clothe yourselves with the Lord Jesus Christ, ...*
*(Romans 13:14, NIV)*

However, leadership can only clothe you with the spiritual clothing that they personally have on. Therefore, make sure the leadership you are following is clothed with Jesus! Paul is an excellent example of one who was clothed with Jesus. That's why he was able to write the Philippians and tell them:

> *Whatever you have learned or received or heard from me, or seen in me—put it into practice. (Philippians 4:9, NIV)*

When the Lord does send you Christlike leadership, receive them and learn how to submit to them. Fulfilling your God-given destiny may hang in the balance based on your submission to the Christlike leadership the Lord sends to prepare you. Elisha had to be willing to submit to and follow Elijah to receive the benefit of his "spiritual covering". Thankfully their relationship blossomed from that point on and was never broken by division or jealousy. In fact, until the time that Elijah was taken by the Lord, Elisha spoke of Elijah as his father.

> *Elisha saw this and cried out, "My father! My father! The chariots and horsemen of Israel!" And Elisha saw him no more. (2 Kings 2:12, NIV)*

### Pause & Reflect

1. The Lord specifically told Elijah to anoint Elisha as the next prophet. Yet there is no mention of Elijah anointing Elisha with oil, which was the typical means of anointing a person. However, Elijah did do something that accomplished the same thing. What was it? (1 Kings 19:19)

2. The throwing of Elijah's cloak around Elisha was a unique way the Lord used to impart the anointing of the Holy Spirit on Elisha. It is important to note that the anointing Elisha received was united with the person he was being called to follow. What does that teach you concerning the anointing Jesus wants to give you?

3. The giving and receiving of Elijah's cloak spoke of the special relationship that Elijah and Elisha would have with one another. What kind of relationship did the Lord want them to have?

4. Why is it important that the leadership you follow is clothed with the Lord Jesus Christ? (Romans 13:14 and Philippians 4:9)

## Disciples Who Become True Sons

Just as Elijah was called by God to become a spiritual father to Elisha, it is also true that Elisha was called to become a spiritual son to Elijah. This served many purposes, but one of the most important was that it prepared Elisha to later fulfill part of Elijah's ministry.

The ministry of a spiritual father is often fulfilled through the lives of his spiritual children. There are many biblical examples of this truth. The promises of God to Abraham were fulfilled through his son, Isaac. The promises God made to Moses were fulfilled through his spiritual son, Joshua. In fact, many of the promises God made to Jesus were and still are being fulfilled through His disciples!

> *Then the disciples went out and preached everywhere, and the Lord worked with them and*

> *confirmed his word by the signs that accompanied it. (Mark 16:20, NIV)*

The Lord had spoken to Elijah to, "anoint Hazael king over Aram."[7] Yet, the Scriptures don't mention Elijah as the one who fulfilled this command but instead tell us that Elisha did![8] The Lord also told Elijah to, "anoint Jehu son of Nimshi king over Israel."[9] However, this wasn't fulfilled by Elijah or Elisha, but by a prophet obeying the command of Elisha!

> *The prophet Elisha summoned a man from the company of the prophets and said to him, "Tuck your cloak into your belt, take this flask of olive oil with you and go to Ramoth Gilead. When you get there, look for Jehu son of Jehoshaphat, the son of Nimshi. Go to him, get him away from his companions and take him into an inner room. Then take the flask and pour the oil on his head and declare, 'This is what the Lord says: I anoint you king over Israel.' Then open the door and run; don't delay!" (2 Kings 9:1-3, NIV)*

That's why Elisha's relationship and submission to Elijah was so important. The Lord was going to use Elisha to finish some of the work that Elijah had originally been given to do. However, in order for that to happen the anointing of Elijah would have to be passed down to Elisha! And in order for that to happen Elisha had to prove himself to be a true spiritual son to Elijah. Thankfully Elisha did and a double portion of Elijah's anointing came upon him. In fact, the anointing that Elisha received not only enabled him to finish Elijah's work but to fulfill God's plan for his own life and ministry.

Another excellent example of disciples who became true sons is found in the account of Gideon and his army.[10] At first Gideon's army numbered 32,000 men. However, the Lord wouldn't allow all those men to follow Gideon into battle for He knew that they would have claimed the victory for themselves. The Lord also knew that most of the men wouldn't be willing to obey the divine directives Gideon would later receive to lead Israel to victory. Therefore, the Lord had to separate the true sons from those who were just casual followers. The Lord whittled the army down to 300 men who proved themselves to be true sons willing to follow Gideon and obey his leadership. Their heart for the Lord and their attitude towards Gideon was seen in their battle cry ...

> *The three companies blew the trumpets and smashed the jars. Grasping the torches in their left hands and holding in their right hands the trumpets they were to blow, they shouted, "A sword for the Lord and for Gideon!" (Judges 7:20, NIV)*

Their declarative battle cry, "A sword for the LORD and for Gideon!" didn't mean they were giving Gideon the Lord's glory or credit for victory. But it does reveal that they were devoted to the LORD and to Gideon as their leader!

Once you've been joined to your spiritual leader prove yourself to be a true spiritual son. Treasure every lesson you are taught and give yourself wholeheartedly to the work you are assigned. You may not understand it all in the beginning, but your call to be a true son to your spiritual leader is God's way of teaching you how to be a disciple of the Lord Jesus.

### *Pause & Reflect*

1. The ministry of a spiritual father is often fulfilled through the lives of his spiritual children. In what ways are some of the promises made to Jesus being fulfilled through His disciples? (Compare Isaiah 49:6, John 14:12, and Mark 16:20)

2. In order to receive Elijah's anointing Elisha had to prove himself to be Elijah's true spiritual son. What was required of Elisha in order to prove this? (2 Kings 2:9-14)

3. In what ways are you proving yourself to be a true spiritual son to your spiritual mentor?

## Disciples Of The Double Portion

When the father of a family died, it was the legal right of the first-born son to receive a double portion of the inheritance, with the rest being equally divided among the remaining children.

> He must acknowledge the son of his unloved wife as the firstborn by giving him a double share of all he has. That son is the first sign of his father's strength. The right of the firstborn belongs to him. (Deuteronomy 21:17, NIV)

The double portion was not a multiplication of all that a person owned, but it did double the inheritance to the first born, which would have set him above his brothers.

Although Elisha was not an actual blood relative of Elijah, he requested the rights of the first born from Elijah. However, he didn't ask for money, land, or anything else in the physical realm. He asked for a double portion of Elijah's *spirit*!

> When they had crossed, Elijah said to Elisha, "Tell me, what can I do for you before I am taken from you?" "Let me inherit a double portion of your spirit," Elisha replied. "You have asked a difficult thing," Elijah said, "yet if you see me when I am taken from you, it will be yours—otherwise, it will not." (2 Kings 2:9-10, NIV)

Elisha had witnessed Elijah to be a man whose spirit was filled with the anointing of the Holy Spirit, and he wanted to be the same type of man! He wanted the same type of prophetic ministry he had seen in Elijah. Elisha knew that if he was to fulfill all that God had called him to do, he was going to need the same type of spirit he had seen in Elijah. A spirit that was humble, hungry for God, open and receptive, filled with faith, overflowing with the anointing of the Holy Spirit, and willing to persevere during the most difficult of circumstances! Yes, in order to fulfill his God given destiny, Elisha was going to need a spirit like Elijah's!

While Elijah told Elisha that his request was a difficult thing, he didn't say that it was an impossible thing for the Lord to give. It all depended on Elisha. If Elisha stayed with Elijah until the end of Elijah's ministry he would receive what he had requested. This is a powerful example showing that you can only receive a double portion from someone that you are submitted to. It also shows the benefit of following the Christlike leadership the Lord gives you! By doing so the anointing of Jesus is going to increase in your own life!

Once again, the anointing of Elijah was given to Elisha through Elijah's cloak.

> *Elisha then picked up Elijah's cloak that had fallen from him and went back and stood on the bank of the Jordan. He took the cloak that had fallen from Elijah and struck the water with it. "Where now is the Lord, the God of Elijah?" he asked. When he struck the water, it divided to the right and to the left, and he crossed over. (2 Kings 2:13–14, NIV)*

As soon as Elisha picked up Elijah's cloak a miraculous ministry began to flow through Elisha that continued to grow as he went about fulfilling the call of God on his life. That which was said to be a "difficult thing" to accomplish was accomplished in Elisha because he had been willing to receive all that God could give him through another person!

The double portion is only available to those who are fully prepared. The necessity of being fully prepared will be dealt with in more detail in section two, but let it be stated here that Elisha was fully prepared to receive the double portion from Elijah.

When Elijah initially called Elisha, it was to finish the race as far as Elijah could take him. However, near the end it seemed as though Elijah was discouraging Elisha from following him any longer.

> *Elijah said to Elisha, "Stay here; the Lord has sent me to Bethel." But Elisha said, "As surely as the Lord lives and as you live, I will not leave you." So they went down to Bethel. ... Then Elijah said to him, "Stay here, Elisha; the Lord has sent me to Jericho." And he replied, "As surely as the Lord lives and as you live, I will not leave you." So they went to Jericho. ... Then Elijah said to him, "Stay here; the Lord has sent me to the Jordan." And he replied, "As surely as the Lord lives and as you live, I will not leave you." So the two of them walked on. (2 Kings 2:2, 4, 6, NIV)*

Three times Elijah told Elisha to, "Stay here" so that Elijah could travel on alone, and each time Elisha answered, "As surely as the LORD lives and as you live, I will not leave you." What was happening here? The Lord was testing Elisha to see if he would be willing to pay the price required to receive the anointing he needed to fulfill his calling. What was that price? Full commitment! In other words, would Elisha be fully committed to the Lord and the leadership God had given to prepare him for ministry?

There were several groups of prophets who knew Elijah was about to be taken by the Lord, but only Elisha followed him to the end. In fact, at both Bethel and Jericho, the prophets talked about what the Lord was about to do, but they showed no interest in being a real part of it. Then at the Jordan River a group of fifty prophets "went and stood at a distance" to watch what God was going to do.

> *The company of the prophets at Bethel came out to Elisha and asked, "Do you know that the Lord is going to take your master from you today?" "Yes, I know," Elisha replied, "so be quiet." ... The company of the prophets at Jericho went up to Elisha and asked him, "Do you know that the Lord is going to take your master from you today?" "Yes, I know," he replied, "so be quiet." ... Fifty men from the company of the prophets went and stood at a distance, facing the place where Elijah and Elisha had stopped at the Jordan. (2 Kings 2:3, 5, 7, NIV)*

This shows that it isn't enough to know the Lord's voice. The company of the prophets heard God's voice but didn't have the desire nor commitment to Elijah to be a part of what God was about to do.

Only Elisha received the double portion that day! In the same way, if you want to receive a double portion, you must fully commit yourself to Jesus and the leadership He will use to prepare you for ministry. Only those who are fully committed can receive a double portion!

Elisha received what he desired from the Lord, yet unfortunately, when he died there was no one found worthy to receive his double portion! This shows that the mantle of ministry doesn't necessarily continue to be passed down from generation to generation. It can and it should be, but Elisha died without being able to impart his ministry into someone else. It wasn't Elisha's fault, nor was it because Elisha didn't have any disciples. Gehazi, the servant of Elisha would surely have been able to receive a great impartation from Elisha, just as Elisha had received from Elijah when he was his servant. However, Gehazi allowed himself to be overtaken by the temptation to profit from his master's ministry. He tried to turn his master's God-given gift into a profitable financial venture.

> *Gehazi, the servant of Elisha the man of God, said to himself, "My master was too easy on Naaman, this Aramean, by not accepting from him what he brought. As surely as the Lord lives, I will run after him and get something from him." (2 Kings 5:20, NIV)*

So instead of receiving an impartation of ministry from his master and mentor, he received God's judgment.[11]

However, Gehazi wasn't the only one who would have been eligible to receive Elisha's double portion. There was also the school of the prophets that looked to Elisha as their leader.

> *The company of the prophets said to Elisha, "Look, the place where we meet with you is too small for us. (2 Kings 6:1, NIV)*

The fact remains that no one was found worthy to receive the ministry of Elisha upon his death. So, when Elisha died the anointing that should have been imparted into others stayed on Elisha's body.

*Once while some Israelites were burying a man, suddenly they saw a band of raiders; so they threw the man's body into Elisha's tomb. When the body touched Elisha's bones, the man came to life and stood up on his feet. (2 Kings 13:21, NIV)*

The Lord Jesus has much to give anyone who is serious about being His disciple. However, in order to receive everything that Jesus wants you to have will require you to submit yourself to the Christlike leaders He brings into your life. Leaders like Elijah who prepared Elisha and through whom Elisha received a "double portion". The double portion anointing is still available, but it's up to you to receive it by answering God's call on your life and fully committing yourself to receive all that Christlike leadership has to give you.

### *Pause & Reflect*

1. What did Elisha mean when he asked Elijah for a double portion of his spirit? (2 Kings 2:9)

2. What made it difficult for Elisha to receive a double portion of Elijah's spirit?

3. In what way was Elisha's loyalty to Elijah severely tested near the end of Elijah's ministry? (2 Kings 2:2-6)

4. In what way(s) was Elisha different from the other prophets in his relationship with Elijah? (2 Kings 2:3-7)

5. What kept Gehazi, Elisha's servant, from receiving an impartation of Elisha's anointing? (2 Kings 5:20-27)

6. What must you do in order to receive an impartation of your spiritual leaders anointing?

## Disciples Who Grow In The Anointing Of Their Leaders

Once Elisha received the anointing of Elijah he had to learn how to flow with that anointing.[12] Thankfully, Elisha not only learned how to flow in Elijah's anointing, but he also began to grow in it.

One of the ways that Elisha grew in the anointing was in the working of miracles. Elisha had seen tremendous miracles in the ministry of Elijah and even began to be used by the Lord in the same way after Elijah was taken to heaven in a chariot of fire. In fact, Scripture records twice as many miracles in the ministry of Elisha than in the ministry of Elijah.

The following is a list of the miracles seen in each of their respective ministries as recorded in Scripture.

**ELIJAH'S MINISTRY**

- **Prophesied Three-Year Drought** (1 Kings 17:1)
- **Multiplied Food** (1 Kings 17:13-16)
- **Raised Boy From The Dead** (1 Kings 17:21-24)
- **Confrontation At Mount Carmel** (1 Kings 18:30-40)
- **Prophesied Rain** (1 Kings 18:41-46)
- **Divine Protection** (2 Kings 1:9-15)
- **Divided The Jordan River** (2 Kings 2:8)

**ELISHA'S MINISTRY**

- **Divided The Jordan River** (2 Kings 2:14)
- **Healed The City's Water Supply** (2 Kings 2:19-22)

- **Pronounced Judgment On Hecklers** (2 Kings 2:23-24)
- **Provision Of Water** (2 Kings 3:15-20)
- **Provision Of Oil** (2 Kings 4:1-7)
- **Raised Boy From The Dead** (2 Kings 4:32-37)
- **Healed Poisonous Food** (2 Kings 4:38-41)
- **Multiplied Food** (2 Kings 4:42-44)
- **Healed Naaman** (2 Kings 5:1-14)
- **Pronounced Judgment On Gehazi** (2 Kings 5:25-27)
- **Caused An Axhead To Float** (2 Kings 6:1-7)
- **Prayed For His Servant To See** (2 Kings 6:17)
- **Victory Over The Aramean Army** (2 Kings 6:18-23)
- **Prophesied The End Of Famine** (2 Kings 7:1-16)

One of the major contributing factors that helped Elisha grow in the anointing was Elijah's ministry that preceded him. The Lord used Elijah's prophetic ministry to help pave the way for Elisha's miraculous ministry. That's right! Elijah helped Elisha grow in the anointing by helping to prepare the way.

While Elisha's ministry was never easy, it was Elijah who had been given the hardest work to accomplish. The Lord had given Elijah the task of moving spiritual mountains, filling in spiritual valleys, and making the crooked spiritual path of his day straight once again. He was able to accomplish this task through his prophetic ministry which enabled him to spiritually, "uproot and tear down, to destroy and overthrow, to build and to plant".[13] Elijah was a trailblazer. He was a mountain mover in the spirit! He was making the way for someone else besides himself. He was preparing the way so that another could come and reap the greater harvest!

A clearer understanding of this aspect of Elijah's ministry can be seen by looking at the ministry of John the Baptist who was sent, "in the spirit and power of Elijah".

> *And he will go on before the Lord, in the spirit and power of Elijah, to turn the hearts of the parents to their children and the disobedient to the wisdom of the righteous—to make ready a people prepared for the Lord. (Luke 1:17, NIV)*

> *As it is written in the book of the words of Isaiah the prophet: "A voice of one calling in the wilderness, 'Prepare the way for the Lord, make straight paths for him. Every valley shall be filled in, every mountain and hill made low. The crooked roads shall become straight, the rough ways smooth. And all people will see God's salvation.'" (Luke 3:4-6, NIV)*

Elisha had the benefit of being able to build upon the solid spiritual foundation that Elijah had already laid. Thus, the growth in the anointing that Elisha experienced was largely due to Elijah who had removed spiritual hindrances and turned the hearts of men back to the Lord.

Another interesting point is that Elijah had been used in the working of miracles and had seen tremendous fruit in that type of ministry. Yet, the fruitfulness that Elisha experienced was double fold! Elijah had, in a spiritual sense, cleared the land, plowed the field, and planted the seed. He saw some of the harvest, but his spiritual son reaped even more! In other words, Elisha was reaping a harvest from the hard labors of Elijah! In the same way, there are many men and women who have plowed the ground and sown the seed for the harvest that you shall reap!

In his teaching about the "sower and the reaper", Jesus confirmed that there would be those like Elijah who would primarily be given the responsibility of preparing the way and sowing the spiritual seed, while others would be sent to reap the greater harvest.

> ... the sower and the reaper may be glad together. Thus the saying 'One sows and another reaps' is true. I sent you to reap what you have not worked for. Others have done the hard work, and you have reaped the benefits of their labor. (John 4:36–38, NIV)

Paul also spoke of this to the Corinthians. He showed how both sowing and reaping are important ministries and that one can't do without the other. In God's Kingdom there should be no jealousy or competition, only cooperation in accomplishing the will of God.

> I planted the seed, Apollos watered it, but God has been making it grow. So neither the one who plants nor the one who waters is anything, but only God, who makes things grow. The one who plants and the one who waters have one purpose, and they will each be rewarded according to their own labor. (1 Corinthians 3:6–8, NIV)

Elijah understood that it was his responsibility to help prepare Elisha in every way possible for the task ahead. Elijah took the responsibility of being Elisha's "spiritual father" very seriously. According to the Law it was his responsibility to impart all that he had into his son.

> *Only be careful, and watch yourselves closely so that you do not forget the things your eyes have seen or let them fade from your heart as long as you live. Teach them to your children and to their children after them.* (Deuteronomy 4:9, NIV)

The principle of this Old Testament law must still be applied today. It is the responsibility of each generation to impart all that they have received from the Lord Jesus into their disciples. But then it is the responsibility of their disciples to keep on growing!

When Jesus gave birth to the Church, it was never His desire for it to stay a baby. It is His will that all of His disciples grow up in Him and become mature.

> *… become mature, attaining to the whole measure of the fullness of Christ.* (Ephesians 4:13, NIV)

That's why you must not be satisfied to merely flow in the anointing of another, as great as that anointing might be. Jesus wants you to learn how to flow in the anointing that you receive from your leadership and then grow in that anointing so that He can be revealed in even greater ways! In that way the scripture will be fulfilled that speaks of the manifestation of the sons of God.

> *For the creation waits with eager longing for the revealing of the sons of God.* (Romans 8:19, ESV)

The work that the Lord has for His Church cannot be accomplished by spiritual babies. It is going to require disciples who have grown up and have become mature "sons". In order for this spiritual growth to take place the Church must build upon the ministry of the first apostles and prophets, but the Church can't stop there! Every disciple of the Lord Jesus must keep on growing until Christ in all His fullness is seen in the Church. I don't believe that God can ever be seen in fullness in just one person, except Jesus Christ Himself. However, I strongly believe that the Church, as the corporate Body of the Lord, is destined to be a full revelation of the Lord Jesus Christ. This will be accomplished as disciples of Jesus receive all they can from their leaders and then keep on growing! That is our call … that is our destiny!

> *And we all, who with unveiled faces contemplate the Lord's glory, are being transformed into his image with ever-increasing glory, … (2 Corinthians 3:18, NIV)*

Thankfully Elisha hungered after God enough to pay the price to grow in the anointing. He wasn't satisfied to stay at the same spiritual level. He knew that there was more, and he was willing to do whatever it would take to receive it and flow in it!

In the same way, disciples who want to grow in the anointing today must have a hunger for more of Jesus and be willing to do whatever is necessary to receive. It is through such disciples that the Lord will be revealed, "with ever-increasing glory!"

### *Pause & Reflect*

1. In what way was Elijah's ministry more difficult than Elisha's?

2. What can be learned about the ministry of Elijah by looking at the ministry of John the Baptist? (Luke 1:17)

3. How can John 4:36-38 be applied to the ministries of Elijah and Elisha?

4. It is the responsibility of each spiritual leader to impart all they have received from the Lord into their disciples. But then it is the responsibility of their disciples to continue growing in the Lord. How was this seen in the mentoring relationship of Elijah and Elisha?

5. In what ways are you growing in the anointing of your mentor?

## Disciples Who Forsake All For The Sake Of The Call

There is a price to be paid by every disciple who desires to fulfill the call of God on his or her life. Thankfully, Elisha was willing to pay the price required of him to become a disciple of Elijah. You read earlier that Elisha, "took his yoke of oxen and slaughtered them. He burned the plowing equipment …."[14] What was Elisha doing? He was burning all of his bridges. He was giving a physical and demonstrative testimony that he was never going to turn back. Thank God for those who are like-hearted and willing to forsake all to follow Jesus and the leadership He gives them. However, while that is a good way to start, you'll soon find out that "burning your bridges" is really just the beginning. For as soon as a disciple puts everything down at the cross to follow Jesus, the enemy will start working on a way to trap and ensnare him! I don't believe that it was long before Elisha faced the temptation to become part of the "religious" crowd. In no way do I want to imply that the "company of prophets" was doing anything wrong. But, if Elisha was to fulfill his calling, he couldn't follow the crowd, even if they were prophets! He could enjoy their fellowship, but he couldn't follow their example. If he had, he would have ceased to follow Elijah and thus would have never taken hold of Elijah's cloak nor received the anointing that came with it!

I have seen this in my own life. I was once the leader of a growing and well-received ministry when the Lord called me to submit myself to an apostle and his ministry. My family and I knew that the Lord was calling us to burn all our ministerial "bridges" behind us. We did so willingly and became fully involved in the apostolic ministry the Lord called us to. Yet, within a year after arriving I was tempted to leave. The ministry was everything that we had hoped that it would be. The presence of the Lord was awesome. The ministry of the Word was the best that we had ever heard, and the vision of our leader was expanding us. But we also started encountering things that we had not anticipated. There is no other way to put it than to say that the Lord started applying the cross to our lives. I thought I had already died to self, but the Lord kept revealing the depth of my selfishness. I was learning that the glory of the Lord always comes with the cross of the Lord! Right in the midst of all of those life changing events and upheavals that involved my entire family I got a call from one of the largest churches I'd ever ministered in, asking me to come and join the staff of their church. I knew that if I did, it would relieve me of all the pressure I had begun to experience (financial, emotional, etc.). But, I had burnt my bridges! There was no turning back. Now, you would think that with such a demonstration of loyalty to my God-appointed leader and to the will of God for my life, that the enemy would leave me alone. Instead that was just the beginning of the tests that were to come. Through the following years I was to be tested time and time again. One of the biggest tests I encountered involved following the crowd. It wasn't the "world" the enemy tried to get me to follow. No, it was the "masses" who also followed the Lord Jesus. But thanks be to God, as the cross was applied to my life, I began to learn that I couldn't fulfill the call of God on my life by following the masses who follow Jesus. I had to follow Jesus with or without anyone else. Yes, it was a lonely road at times, but I was learning that no matter how wonderful the crowd may be, they can't take the place of Jesus!

You have to get to the point that you realize that the crowds don't have what you're hungering for ... only Jesus does! There will always be the masses who follow Jesus. But what will you do if the crowd ceases to follow Him?

# CALLED TO BE DISCIPLES

> *On hearing it, many of his disciples said, "This is a hard teaching. Who can accept it?" Aware that his disciples were grumbling about this, Jesus said to them, "Does this offend you? ... From this time many of his disciples turned back and no longer followed him. "You do not want to leave too, do you?" Jesus asked the Twelve. Simon Peter answered him, "Lord, to whom shall we go? You have the words of eternal life. We have come to believe and to know that you are the Holy One of God." (John 6:60-61, 66-69, NIV)*

It's great when the crowds follow Jesus, but don't fall into the trap of just being part of a crowd, even a Christian crowd. You are an individual who must make an individual choice. With or without the crowds, no matter what it takes, you must take your stand and say, "I'm going to follow Jesus!"

In Scripture you'll never read about a follower of the crowds doing the works of Jesus. Many people in the crowds received miracles from Jesus, but they are never mentioned as doing miracles in His Name. Yet, you do read of the signs, wonders, and miracles that followed the disciples who forsook all to follow Jesus!

> *Then the disciples went out and preached everywhere, and the Lord worked with them and confirmed his word by the signs that accompanied it. (Mark 16:20, NIV)*

> *So Paul and Barnabas spent considerable time there, speaking boldly for the Lord, who confirmed the message of his grace by enabling them to perform signs and wonders. (Acts 14:3, NIV)*

Jesus is calling you to become His disciple … a sold-out disciple! One who will serve Him willingly and doesn't have to be begged. One who will be receptive to the anointing and who is willing to forsake all for the sake of the call. Others have heard His call and made their choice. Now the Lord is awaiting your answer. I pray that you will rise and follow the call of the Lord.

### *Pause & Reflect*

1. Explain how your life has changed since you accepted the call of Jesus Christ to be His disciple?

2. Since you have dedicated yourself to being a disciple of Jesus Christ what have you done to overcome the temptation to slack off?

---

1. 1 Kings 19:1-4
2. John 15:5 (ESV)
3. Luke 14:27-30 (ESV)
4. Nelson's Illustrated Bible Dictionary, Biblesoft Electronic Database. Copyright ©1986 by Thomas Nelson Publishers. All rights reserved.
5. Brown Driver & Briggs Hebrew Lexicon, Biblesoft Electronic Database. Copyright © 1993 by Woodside Bible Fellowship, Ontario, Canada.
6. 1 Corinthians 1:28-29
7. 1 Kings 19:15 (NIV)
8. 2 Kings 8:7–15
9. 1 Kings 19:16 (NIV)
10. Judges 7
11. 2 Kings 5:26–27
12. 1 John 2:27
13. Jeremiah 1:10 (NIV)
14. 1 Kings 19:21 (NIV)

# Chapter Two

# Called To Be Ministers Of The Old & New Wine

There was no greater minister in Israel than Elijah when God called Elisha to become his disciple. Elijah was a unique instrument of the Lord sent to God's people with a message of repentance that was demonstrated with awesome signs, wonders, and miracles.[1] It was a privilege to have been called by the Lord to follow such a mighty man of God.

What was it in Elisha that attracted the Lord to call him to such a ministry? I believe that one of the basic reasons was that Elisha shared Elijah's hunger for God! That is a key to being used by God in ministry. It is not just a matter of knowing the truth and walking in the righteous path of the Lord. You must hunger for more and more of God! I believe that Elisha did and thus was able to follow Elijah in his powerful and unique ministry.

## Satisfied With The Familiar?

In the last chapter it was mentioned that the "company of the LORD's prophets" were active in ministry at the time of Elijah. Although scripture does not directly indicate who their leader was, Elijah would most likely have been considered the head prophet among them. He certainly would have had input into their lives. In fact, Elijah's close relationship with them is seen in that he visited each group before he was taken to Heaven.[2] Unfortunately, although the company of prophets knew that the Lord was about to do something tremendous, they were satisfied to be onlookers instead of active participants. Only one person had enough hunger for God to stay with Elijah until the end, and that was Elisha.

In the same way there are those today who have great knowledge of the Lord and His work. Yet, it's never enough for the Church to know about the Lord and what He is doing. The Lord wants His disciples to be active participants in what He is doing! That was one of the main differences between Elisha and the company of prophets. They both had knowledge, but Elisha's spiritual hunger for God drove him to step out of the familiar to receive all that the Lord had for him.

It was that type of spiritual hunger that I believe gave Peter the desire to step out of the boat into the water to follow Jesus.

> "Lord, if it's you," Peter replied, "tell me to come to you on the water." "Come," he said. Then Peter got down out of the boat, walked on the water and came toward Jesus. (Matthew 14:28–29, NIV)

Peter could have stayed in the boat with familiar surroundings. Yet, seeing Jesus walking on the water revealed to Peter that there was more of Jesus that he was not experiencing. He wanted to be a part of everything Jesus was doing. He wasn't satisfied to see Jesus walk on water, he wanted to do it with Him! Peter's hunger drove him out of the boat onto unfamiliar territory and took him closer to Jesus! Peter would have stayed in the boat had Jesus told him to, but thank God, Jesus said, "Come". The Lord is telling disciples once more to step out of their familiar surroundings and walk with Him in the miraculous! That is part of your calling. That is your destiny. You have been called to minister in the power and authority of the Holy Spirit just like Jesus! But, first you must hunger for more of God like Elisha did. You can't be satisfied with the familiar. You have to be willing to step out of your comfort zone just like Peter did. You have to have such a spiritual hunger for more of Jesus that you're willing to do whatever is necessary to receive! It is this type of spiritual hunger that will be the propelling force in those who will be used by God in these last days; a hunger for more of Jesus that calls you beyond the familiar into true Christlike ministry with signs and wonders following. Such a hunger will always be open to "new wine".

### *Pause & Reflect*

1. The "company of the Lord's prophets" most likely looked at Elijah as their leader, but they did not have the same type of relationship with him that Elisha did. How did Elisha differ from the "company of the Lord's prophets" in his relationship with Elijah?

2. In 2 Kings 2:5 we are told that the company of prophets knew something tremendous was about to happen to Elijah, yet they were satisfied to be onlookers instead of active participants. Only one person had enough hunger for God to stay with Elijah until the end, and that was Elisha. Evaluate your life; are you like Elisha who was receiving all that God was giving him or are you more like the company of prophets who "stood at a distance"? (2 Kings 2:7)

3. In what way did Peter reveal in Matthew 14:28-29 that he wanted to experience life with Jesus to the fullest?

4. In what way(s) are you answering the call of Jesus to step out of your comfort zone and walk with Him in the miraculous?

## "Old Wine" And "New Wine"

"Old wine" in the Bible is symbolic of revelations of truth the Lord has given His people in the past, while "new wine" is symbolic of fresh revelation of truth. "Old wine" is also related to the previous things the Lord has done, while "new wine" is related to the present manifestation of the Lord.

"Old wine" must never be viewed as without purpose or worth for our present day. However, the Church must be careful not to reject new revelation from the Lord Jesus. In God's Kingdom, both "old and new wine" are needed to develop Christlike lives and ministries. It is through the ministry of both that the Church will become whole and mature. For example, the early New Testament Christians would never have thought of the ministries of Abraham, Moses, David, Elijah, or Elisha as having no significance to their lives and ministries. Yet, they realized that they needed "new wine" if they were to go forward and accomplish what Jesus had given them to do. Thankfully, the New Testament Church was open to both the "old and new wine"! In fact, the ministry of the early apostles was so effective because they were grounded in the "old wine" of their forefathers, but were receptive vessels of "new wine".

Jesus taught that the old treasures of revelation and ministry have a purpose alongside the new treasures He will give the Church.

> He said to them, "Therefore every teacher of the law who has become a disciple in the kingdom of heaven is like the owner of a house who brings out of his storeroom new treasures as well as old." (Matthew 13:52, NIV)

However, you mustn't confuse old traditions with old truths. Jesus taught a parable about the "new wine" and "old wineskins" that will help you see the difference between the two.

> Neither do people pour new wine into old wineskins. If they do, the skins will burst; the wine will run out and the wineskins will be ruined. No, they pour new wine into new wineskins, and both are preserved. (Matthew 9:17, NIV)

"Wineskins" are used to carry the wine. Old wineskins symbolize previous methods, traditions, or even people that the Lord used to accomplish a work in His Kingdom. For a season, people may be followed, methods may be taught, and traditions may be repeated, but they must never be thought of in the same way as the Lord's truth. Never forget that the wine is more important than the wineskin! People, methods, and traditions change, but truth and principles last forever.

Jesus taught that traditions will not stretch to accommodate the fresh revelation of truth He will bring to the Church to accomplish His work. That's why you may have to discard "old wineskins" (methods), but you must treasure "old wine" (truth and ministry that has been previously revealed) as valuable. "Old wine" is needed because it will often help you understand the present revelations the Lord continues to give today.

An example of the difference between truth and methodology is seen in the many different "methods" Jesus used in His healing ministry. In one instance He put mud made from His saliva on the eyes of a blind man.

> *After saying this, he spit on the ground, made some mud with the saliva, and put it on the man's eyes. "Go," he told him, "wash in the Pool of Siloam" (this word means "Sent"). So the man went and washed, and came home seeing. (John 9:6–7, NIV)*

However, the Lord didn't continue to repeat this method to heal the blind. Jesus was open to being used in this way even though it was a bit unusual, but He didn't create a tradition from this occurrence. Jesus didn't start spitting on everybody! The truth revealed was that God heals, even though the methods Jesus used to heal varied. As far as "methods" are concerned: you need to hold on to the truth conveyed by the method, not the method itself. Unfortunately, too many have held tenaciously to "methods" while losing sight of the truth they were supposed to impart! That's why traditions practiced in the Church without the leading of the Holy Spirit will never produce life. Traditions in the Church have had their place in the past and will continue to do so in the present, helping provide form and structure. However, when Jesus gives His Church fresh revelation of truth that the old traditions won't accommodate, the old traditions must be discarded.

Jesus warned His disciples of the tendency people have of rejecting anything new because they have become accustomed and satisfied with the old and familiar.

> *And no one after drinking old wine wants the new, for they say, 'The old is better.' (Luke 5:39, NIV)*

# CALLED TO BE MINISTERS OF THE OLD & NEW WINE

For example, Elijah's ministry had been a constant reminder of the new things God could do through those who were willing. He was a vessel filled with "new wine" from the Lord. However, when Elijah was taken by the Lord, that which had been "new wine" to him became "old wine" to those he left behind. Thankfully, Elisha had learned from Elijah to stay open to fresh revelation. After Elijah was taken by the Lord Elisha began to receive and flow with "new wine". Elijah's ministry wasn't to be forgotten, but it wasn't to be idolized either. The company of prophets knew God had started something new. They had seen for themselves the mantle of anointing given to Elisha. They had even seen the results of the anointing which was flowing through Elisha. Unfortunately, they preferred "old wine". They wanted to hold onto that which was familiar to them! It's sad that it wasn't until the Lord took Elijah that the company of the prophets wanted to look for him. They hadn't been willing to leave their area of familiarity before, but when Elijah was taken from them they wanted him back and did all they could to find him!

> "Look," they said, "we your servants have fifty able men. Let them go and look for your master. Perhaps the Spirit of the Lord has picked him up and set him down on some mountain or in some valley." "No," Elisha replied, "do not send them." (2 Kings 2:16, NIV)

### Pause & Reflect

1. What was Jesus referring to in Matthew 13:52 when He taught that the Kingdom of Heaven has both old and new treasures.

2. What was Jesus referring to in Matthew 9:17 when He spoke of "old wineskins"?

3. In Matthew 9:17 what did the "new wine" symbolize?

4. Give an example of a unique method of ministry used by Jesus.

5. Why is it important for the Church to embrace both "old wine" and "new wine"?

## Your Attitude Towards "Old Wine"

So, what should your attitude be towards truth and ministry that has been revealed in the past? Remember it!

> *Remember the former things, those of long ago; I am God, and there is no other; I am God, and there is none like me. (Isaiah 46:9, NIV)*

The truth received by and proven in the lives of saints before you will be a great help to you. Their lives and ministries are like a road map that will help keep you on the right path. In fact, you not only need to remember the truth taught in previous generations, you need to teach it.

> *Only be careful, and watch yourselves closely so that you do not forget the things your eyes have seen or let them fade from your heart as long as you live. Teach them to your children and to their children after them. (Deuteronomy 4:9, NIV)*

It would be unwise to disregard what the Lord taught godly leaders of the past. The lessons they learned and taught are needed by every disciple in every generation. However, while you remember their lives and ministries and the truths that they taught, you don't want to become spiritually stagnate! That's why the Lord also gave

Isaiah a prophecy telling Israel to forget the former things He had done in their midst.

> *"Forget the former things; do not dwell on the past. See, I am doing a new thing! Now it springs up; do you not perceive it? I am making a way in the wilderness and streams in the wasteland. (Isaiah 43:18-19, NIV)*

Why would the Lord tell His people to both "forget the former things" and then to "remember the former things"? The Lord was dealing with man's tendency to stagnate over time. In the past the Lord had delivered His people from their bondage in Egypt and had miraculously taken them through the Red Sea on dry ground. Yet, God's people needed deliverance during the time that Isaiah was ministering. The Lord didn't want Isaiah's generation to die with memories of what He used to do. He was ready to move in their present situation with power and deliverance. So, the Lord reminded Israel of what He had done in their past to build their faith and expectancy for Him to move in their present situation. God told them that they couldn't rest on their spiritual heritage, they had to experience Him in their present circumstances! They couldn't rest solely on what they had learned in the past, they had to have a fresh revelation of the Lord in their midst! The Lord is telling His disciples the same thing today. Don't be satisfied with what you've learned about Jesus in the past. Be open to a fresh revelation of the life and ministry of Jesus in the present!

The Lord was also telling Israel to remember the truth and the ministry of yesterday, but don't hang onto the methods. In the same way, you must be open to the new ways the Lord will move in your midst. The Lord is going to raise up disciples using new methods to glorify and lift up Jesus to a new generation. You'd better be open, or you'll miss God! The Lord is always doing a new thing using new "wineskins" to hold the new wine He is pouring into the Church. So, be thankful for your spiritual heritage and the stability you have received from it, but Jesus has more "wine" He wants to give the Church! Just as He told His disciples: "I have much more to say to you, more than you can now bear. But when he, the Spirit of truth, comes, he will guide you into all the truth. ..." (John 16:12–13, NIV). Therefore, if you're going to receive more of Jesus you have to be open to the Holy Spirit to lead you into a greater revelation of Jesus!

### *Pause & Reflect*

1. What should your attitude be towards truth and ministry that was revealed in the past? (Isaiah 46:9)

2. Why would it be unwise to disregard what the Lord taught godly leaders of the past?

3. In Isaiah 46:9 (NIV) the Lord said, "Remember the former things, those of long ago;" yet in Isaiah 43:18-19 (NIV) we are told, "Forget the former things; do not dwell on the past." Compare these two passages; explain what they mean and how you can apply them to your life.

## The Power Released In "New Wine"

There is a tremendous amount of power released in "new wine" during the early stages of fermentation. In the climate of Palestine, the fermentation of newly pressed grapes begins almost immediately. In fact, fermentation never begins later than the next day after the juice has been extracted from the grapes. At first, a slight foam appears on the surface of the liquid. Then the action rapidly becomes more violent. At the beginning of the fermentation process the new wine must be kept in jars or in a vat, for it would burst even the newest and strongest of wineskins. Within about a week this violent fermentation subsides, and the wine is transferred to other jars or strong wineskins where the power of fermentation continues to do its work. Only at the end of forty days is the fermented wine drawn off into other jars or wineskins in order to preserve it.

This process of fermentation gives a powerful object lesson of what happens in the spiritual realm when the Lord gives His Church a fresh revelation of Himself. An excellent example of this is what happened on the Day of Pentecost when the disciples were baptized with the Holy Spirit. Approximately three thousand were added to the Church that day, yet that was just the beginning.[3] Within days thousands more became followers of Jesus and were added to the Church!

> But many who heard the message believed; so the number of men who believed grew to about five thousand. (Acts 4:4, NIV)

The revelation of Jesus that was given to the early Church was overflowing with power, just like new wine that is beginning to ferment. And because the early Church devoted themselves to receiving everything the Lord had for them, the power of the new wine continued to flow in their midst!

> They devoted themselves to the apostles' teaching and to fellowship, to the breaking of bread and to prayer. Everyone was filled with awe at the many wonders and signs performed by the apostles. (Acts 2:42-43, NIV)

However, less than one hundred years later there was a marked decline in the Church's power. To the local church in Laodicea, Jesus had John the Apostle write these words:

> *I know your deeds, that you are neither cold nor hot. I wish you were either one or the other! So, because you are lukewarm—neither hot nor cold—I am about to spit you out of my mouth. You say, 'I am rich; I have acquired wealth and do not need a thing.' But you do not realize that you are wretched, pitiful, poor, blind and naked. (Revelation 3:15-17, NIV)*

What happened? Many things were involved, but one of them was that the Church had ceased to receive "new wine!" Whenever the Church ceases to receive "new wine" it begins to decline spiritually, morally, and in effectiveness.

Unfortunately, when "new wine" is being poured out there are those who try to categorize it, conform it, organize it, and tame it into something less threatening. The result? The wine becomes so diluted and distorted that it no longer reveals the life of Jesus it was given to convey. Such "wine" may keep its "form of godliness", but it no longer contains its previous life changing power![4]

The Church desperately needs the power of "new wine" in order to carry out its mission. However, that doesn't mean that there's no life and power in "old wine". Far from it! As long as "old wine" is kept pure and not mixed with man's own ideas and traditions there will be life in it.[5] But if the Church wants to grow, "in the knowledge of the Son of God and become mature, attaining to the whole measure of the fullness of Christ"[6] it needs to be receptive to "new wine". Each generation must receive a fuller revelation of Jesus than their predecessors. They in turn will be responsible to impart what they have received into the next generation. Therefore, each generation builds upon the foundation of the previous generation, yet strives to receive more! In that way the Church will grow in Christlikeness and the glory revealed in the Church will increase until it is a revelation of Jesus Christ in His fullness!

*And we all, who with unveiled faces contemplate the Lord's glory, are being transformed into his image with ever-increasing glory, which comes from the Lord, who is the Spirit. (2 Corinthians 3:18, NIV)*

When Jesus came He brought with Him old and new wine (symbolically). It was through the use of both (truth previously revealed in the Old Testament and fresh revelation) that Jesus revealed Himself. As He revealed Himself, lives were changed! The Word was being revealed in purity and power. Man was seeing the Word as it really is ... alive, active, and powerful![7]

*He went to Nazareth, where he had been brought up, and on the Sabbath day he went into the synagogue, as was his custom. He stood up to read, and the scroll of the prophet Isaiah was handed to him. Unrolling it, he found the place where it is written: "The Spirit of the Lord is on me, because he has anointed me to proclaim good news to the poor. He has sent me to proclaim freedom for the prisoners and recovery of sight for the blind, to set the oppressed free, to proclaim the year of the Lord's favor." Then he rolled up the scroll, gave it back to the attendant and sat down. The eyes of everyone in the synagogue were fastened on him. He began by saying to them, "Today this scripture is fulfilled in your hearing." (Luke 4:16-21, NIV)*

*Jesus went through all the towns and villages, teaching in their synagogues, proclaiming the good news of the kingdom and healing every disease and sickness. (Matthew 9:35, NIV)*

> *... God anointed Jesus of Nazareth with the Holy Spirit and power, and how he went around doing good and healing all who were under the power of the devil, because God was with him. (Acts 10:38, NIV)*

The revelation of Jesus is what the "wine" is all about. The "old wine" will give you perspective and balance as you learn from the past and the "new wine" will make you a powerful, effective, and fruitful witness for Jesus! So, it was never meant to be one or the other. Both are needed to development solid disciples for Jesus!

### Pause & Reflect

1. In what way is the fermentation process of "new wine" a spiritual object lesson to the Church?

2. What must the disciples of Jesus Christ do to keep the power of "new wine" flowing in their midst?

3. In what ways does the Church decline when it ceases to flow in "new wine"?

4. What will keep "old wine" from revealing the life of the Lord?

5. What must each generation of the Church do to grow, "in the knowledge of the Son of God and become mature, attaining to the whole measure of the fullness of Christ"? (Ephesians 4:13, NIV)

6. Explain the benefits of both "old wine" and "new wine" and why the Church needs both.

## The "Old" And "New" Working Together

The Church seems to lean towards one of two extremes regarding revelation and ministry. There are those who are closed to any new revelation of truth and ministry, and there are those who are always running after something new and different. Obviously, both extremes are wrong and must be avoided. So, how do you achieve a balance? You must hold on to the old and be open to the new. Elisha held on to the old by taking up the cloak of Elijah. In fact, he continued to use the cloak of Elijah in his ministry. He wasn't quick to discard the "old" just to be independent and free. Elisha realized that his ministry was a continuation of the "wine" that had previously been flowing through Elijah. But Elisha didn't make the cloak an idol either. Unfortunately, man is tempted to make the "old" an idol. That's why King Hezekiah had to destroy the bronze snake Moses made in the wilderness. The bronze snake had previously been used by the Lord to bring healing to the children of Israel. It was a symbol of Jesus, who by taking our sin upon Himself became our Healer. But the nation of Israel took the old symbol and idolized it!

> *He broke into pieces the bronze snake Moses had made, for up to that time the Israelites had been burning incense to it. (It was called Nehushtan.) (2 Kings 18:4, NIV)*

Thankfully, you have a good example to follow in Elisha. He continued to walk in the power of the "old" but didn't allow it to become an idol in his life. He was open to other ways the Lord might move. Likewise, you need to learn from the past, but you mustn't allow yourself to think that God can only move with "old wine". As a minister in God's Kingdom, you are called to work with both! You must hold on to the "old" that will give you a spiritual foundation, a spiritual barometer, a starting point. But you must also continue to receive the "new" that builds upon the "old".

An excellent example of this is found in the way Jesus ministered with both "old and new wine". Jesus gave two men new revelation from Old Testament Scriptures that they had known and studied all of their lives. Jesus gave them "new wine", but He based it on the "old wine" they had previously been given.

> *And beginning with Moses and all the Prophets, he explained to them what was said in all the Scriptures concerning himself. ... They asked each other, "Were not our hearts burning within us while he talked with us on the road and opened the Scriptures to us?" (Luke 24:27, 32, NIV)*

Paul the Apostle was also one who never discarded the "old wine". He understood the value and necessity of knowing what God had done in the past. The old truths he had learned as a child gave him a foundation and a reference point for understanding the will and ways of God. Yet, he didn't allow old truth to keep him from receiving further revelation.

> *I want you to know, brothers and sisters, that the gospel I preached is not of human origin. I did not receive it from any man, nor was I taught it; rather, I received it by revelation from Jesus Christ. (Galatians 1:11-12, NIV)*

Paul realized that "old wine" and "new wine" are supposed to work together because the goal of both is to reveal Jesus. In fact, Jesus is the essence of both. The purpose of the "old wine" (that which has been tried and proven and gives stability) is to reveal Jesus. Likewise, the purpose of the "new wine" (that which keeps the Church growing) is also to reveal Jesus. There is no contradiction between the two! Both the "old wine" and "new wine" are revelations of Jesus as revealed by the Spirit in the Word!

Therefore, hold onto the "old wine" but stay hungry for the "new wine" for you have been called by God to be a minister of both!

### *Pause & Reflect*

1. What two extremes has the Church fallen into throughout Church history?

2. What did Elisha do that helped him avoid these two extremes in ministry?

3. Give an example of how Jesus exemplified balance in His ministry.

4. Explain how the Apostle Paul was a minister of both the "old wine" and "new wine".

---

1. That is not to say that Elijah was the only one the Lord was using at that time. The Bible mentions others who stood faithfully with the Lord when the nation of Israel had, for the most part, turned to idolatry through Baal worship. See 1 Kings 19:18
2. 2 Kings 2:3-7
3. Acts 2:41
4. 2 Timothy 3:5 (NIV)
5. Mark 7:7-8
6. Ephesians 4:13 (NIV)
7. Hebrews 4:12 (NIV)

# Chapter Three

# Called To Demonstrate The Gospel Of Jesus Christ

What does it mean to demonstrate the gospel of Jesus Christ? To demonstrate the gospel in power is to give people a true revelation of who Jesus is and what He is like. While much can be said about representing Jesus in your life and ministry, this chapter will concentrate on presenting the gospel to others with the visual manifestation of God's power. That was the type of ministry Paul had and which he referred to in his letter to the Corinthians.

> *My message and my preaching were not with wise and persuasive words, but with a demonstration of the Spirit's power, ... (1 Corinthians 2:4, NIV)*

There is no greater manifestation of the Spirit's power than when people are "born again" and experience a complete change in their lives. Yet, Jesus desires mankind to experience the power of God in other ways as well. Healings, deliverance, and miracles were just as much a part of the ministry of Jesus as preaching and teaching the Word.

> *"The Spirit of the Lord is on me, because he has anointed me to proclaim good news to the poor. He has sent me to proclaim freedom for the prisoners and recovery of sight for the blind, to set the oppressed free, to proclaim the year of the Lord's favor." (Luke 4:18–19, NIV)*

As you read the Gospels you will continuously see how Jesus did more than preach and teach the Word of God, He demonstrated the reality of it! Everywhere Jesus went He reached out to others and miraculously intervened in their lives as they came to Him for help. And as Jesus raised up disciples He commissioned them to carry out the same type of ministry.

> *The seventy-two returned with joy and said, "Lord, even the demons submit to us in your name." He replied, "I saw Satan fall like lightning from heaven. I have given you authority to trample on snakes and scorpions and to overcome all the power of the enemy; nothing will harm you." (Luke 10:17–19, NIV)*

The New Testament Church knew that preaching the Gospel without having it confirmed with signs, wonders, and miracles wouldn't be a true representation of the life and ministry of Jesus. That's why they weren't hesitant to ask the Lord to reveal His mighty hand in miraculous ways!

> *Stretch out your hand to heal and perform signs and wonders through the name of your holy servant Jesus. (Acts 4:30, NIV)*

Needless to say, the Lord continued to answer their prayers!

> *The apostles performed many signs and wonders among the people. (Acts 5:12, NIV)*

> *So Paul and Barnabas spent considerable time there, speaking boldly for the Lord, who confirmed the message of his grace by enabling them to perform signs and wonders. (Acts 14:3, NIV)*

> *This salvation, which was first announced by the Lord, was confirmed to us by those who heard him. God also testified to it by signs, wonders and various miracles, and by gifts of the Holy Spirit distributed according to his will. (Hebrews 2:3-4, NIV)*

But miraculous ministry is by no means limited to the New Testament! The Lord has always revealed Himself in miraculous ways. Thank God He isn't going to change!

> *Jesus Christ is the same yesterday and today and forever. (Hebrews 13:8, NIV)*

So, what is it going to take for present day disciples of Jesus to minister in the miraculous? What do you have to do to have the Lord confirm His Word through you with signs, wonders, and miracles? Let's look at the life of Elisha, for he is an excellent example of a disciple who not only asked these questions but also found the answers!

## Elisha Desired To Demonstrate God's Power

Since Elisha was a disciple of Elijah he was aware of the many ways God had used Elijah. He knew that Elijah had prophesied drought over Israel, that he was fed by ravens at Cherith, that the Lord used him to raise the widow's son back to life, and that he had triumphantly confronted the prophets of Baal on Mt. Carmel. While the Bible isn't clear about the specific miracles Elisha got to witness as he followed Elijah, this much is known, it did nurture a spiritual hunger in Elisha. That's why, when Elisha saw Elijah go to heaven in a chariot of fire he cried out,

> "Where now is the Lord, the God of Elijah?" (2 Kings 2:14, NIV)

That wasn't just a cry for the Lord to reveal Himself. Elisha had seen the Lord reveal Himself through Elijah and he wanted to see the same thing in his own life and ministry!

Elisha knew that when the Lord spoke through Elijah it resulted in revelation and manifestation. Thus, he had learned to expect a demonstration of the Spirit's power whenever the word of the Lord was spoken. In other words, Elisha wasn't going to be satisfied to just preach the word of the Lord, he wanted to see God's word demonstrated through the power of the Holy Spirit! Elisha wasn't disappointed, and neither will you be if you hunger after God like Elisha did, for there was an immediate demonstration of the Spirit's power as Elisha struck the Jordan River with the cloak he had received from Elijah.

> He took the cloak that had fallen from Elijah and struck the water with it. "Where now is the Lord, the God of Elijah?" he asked. When he struck the water,

> *it divided to the right and to the left, and he crossed over. (2 Kings 2:14, NIV)*

However, the demonstration of the Spirit's power isn't always evident in the physical realm when you declare God's word. The word of the Lord is always powerful and effective and it will always accomplish God's purpose. But the work that it accomplishes may be in the spiritual realm and thus unseen by the natural eye. Therefore, when you declare God's word always anticipate the demonstration of the Spirit's power, but be aware that it won't always be visible to the natural eye. So, whether or not you see a demonstration of the Spirit's power in the physical realm when you declare the word of the Lord continue to declare it by faith, for it is accomplishing great things in the spiritual realm that will eventually be manifested in the physical realm!

> *As the rain and the snow come down from heaven, and do not return to it without watering the earth and making it bud and flourish, so that it yields seed for the sower and bread for the eater, so is my word that goes out from my mouth: It will not return to me empty, but will accomplish what I desire and achieve the purpose for which I sent it. (Isaiah 55:10–11, NIV)*

### Pause & Reflect

1. What does it mean to demonstrate the gospel of Jesus Christ?

2. What are some of the ways that Jesus demonstrated the power of God? (Luke 4:18-19)

3. What are some of the miraculous ways that Jesus wants His gospel to be demonstrated by His disciples today? (Luke 10:17-19; Acts 14:3; Hebrews 2:3-4)

4. Explain why Elisha cried out, "Where now is the LORD, the God of Elijah?" (2 Kings 2:14, NIV)

5. How should you deal with the fact that a demonstration of the Spirit's power is not always evident in the physical realm when you declare God's word by faith? (Isaiah 55:10-11)

## It Takes The Cross To Demonstrate The Gospel

It has already been mentioned that Elisha had a desire to demonstrate the word of the Lord through the power of the Holy Spirit. However, it takes more than desire to reach fulfillment, you've got to be willing to pay the price to bring your desires to fruition. Thankfully, Elisha paid the price! As a disciple and aide to Elijah he embraced a life of self-denial, humility, and discipline. Elisha's choice to obey God by serving Elijah led to his transformation and prepared him for his future ministry. That's why when the anointing came on him to flow in the miraculous, he was ready!

That's why Jesus told His disciples that if they wanted to follow Him they would have to carry a cross, which was symbolic of living a life of self-denial. Jesus knew that dying to self was a prerequisite to picking up the cloak of true ministry. In other words, resurrection power only flows after the cross is applied! In fact, the centrality of the cross is at the very heart of the gospel that Jesus proclaimed.

> *Then he said to them all: "Whoever wants to be my disciple must deny themselves and take up their cross daily and follow me." (Luke 9:23, NIV)*

That's one of the reasons why the Lord was able to use Paul in such powerful ways. The Apostle Paul didn't run from the cross, instead he embraced it. He became one with Christ on His cross!

> *I have been crucified with Christ and I no longer live, but Christ lives in me. The life I now live in the body, I live by faith in the Son of God, who loved me and gave himself for me. (Galatians 2:20, NIV)*

It's wonderful if you have a desire for God to use you in the miraculous. However, if you're not daily allowing the cross to be applied to your life, the desire to be used by God can often become self-serving. Simon was such a man. He saw Philip and the apostles being used in miraculous ways and he wanted the same power and ministry manifesting in his own life.

> *Simon himself believed and was baptized. And he followed Philip everywhere, astonished by the great signs and miracles he saw. … When Simon saw that the Spirit was given at the laying on of the apostles' hands, he offered them money and said, "Give me also this ability so that everyone on whom I lay my hands may receive the Holy Spirit." Peter answered: "May your money perish with you, because you thought you could buy the gift of God with money! You have no part or share in this ministry, because your heart is not right before God. Repent of this wickedness and pray to the Lord in the hope that he may forgive you for having such a thought in your heart. For I see that you are full of bitterness and captive to sin." (Acts 8:13, 18–23, NIV)*

# CALLED TO DEMONSTRATE THE GOSPEL OF JESUS CHRIST

Simon desired to have a miraculous ministry, but not for the right reasons. It wasn't for God's glory that he desired it; it was for his own. He had failed to embrace the cross. Thus, his selfish desires continued to motivate and lead him towards destruction! That's why it is absolutely necessary that every disciple keep the cross of Jesus at the center of his or her life. The power of your sinful nature is too strong for you to ignore. It's only when you become one with Christ on His cross that you'll find true freedom in Christ.

The importance of the cross in the life of a disciple is clearly seen in Paul's reference to those who were, "enemies of the cross of Christ".

> *For, as I have often told you before and now tell you again even with tears, many live as enemies of the cross of Christ. Their destiny is destruction, their god is their stomach, and their glory is in their shame. Their mind is set on earthly things. (Philippians 3:18-19, NIV)*

Notice that Paul didn't say that the people he was referring to hated Jesus, they just hated His cross! I believe the same could have been said of Simon. He thought he loved Jesus, but because he was unwilling to die to himself, his sinful desires for self-glorification had not been dealt with. He didn't realize that Christlike ministry and the cross always go together.

Elisha is an excellent example of one who was willing to sacrifice his own will in order to serve the Lord. In New Testament terminology it could be said that Elisha took up his "cross" and allowed the Lord to have His way in his life. You don't read of Elisha ever complaining about the sacrifices he made to be a disciple of Elijah. He was a man that died to "self" and by doing so was prepared to minister with the power of God! That's what your "cross" will accomplish in your life if you take it up and follow Jesus.

### Pause & Reflect

1. Why was the Lord able to give Elisha such a powerful and miraculous ministry?

2. Why is dying to self a prerequisite to true Christlike ministry? (Reference Luke 9:23)

3. Simon was a man in the New Testament who desired to have a miraculous ministry, but not for the right reasons. What was wrong with his motives and what did he fail to do that revealed the corruption in his heart? (Acts 8:13-24)

4. What must you do to keep your heart right and your motives pure as God begins to use you in miraculous ways?

5. Explain what the Apostle Paul meant when he wrote "many live as enemies of the cross of Christ." (Philippians 3:18, NIV)

## Receiving Impartation From Your Leadership

Elisha embraced the life that he saw exemplified in the life of Elijah; a life that was totally surrendered to the Lord. By doing so Elisha began to receive from Elijah the impartation, preparation, and faith that he would one day need to demonstrate the word of the Lord. This once again shows the need for all disciples of Jesus to be under leadership who are Christlike in life and ministry. It is through such leadership that Jesus imparts spiritual gifts into His disciples and prepares them for effective and fruitful service in the Kingdom of God. By submitting to Christlike leaders your life and ministry will never be the same!

# CALLED TO DEMONSTRATE THE GOSPEL OF JESUS CHRIST

But notice, Elisha didn't just receive ministry from Elijah ... he received the "spirit of Elijah". In other words, the ministry that had been seen in Elijah was imparted into Elisha. That was possible because Elisha was willing to die to himself and embrace what the Lord was giving him through Elijah. In the same way the Lord will use your leadership to impart into you (through the ministry of the Word, prophecy, prayer, etc.) that which you need to fulfill your calling. You can expect that the Lord will impart into you the same qualities that you see in your leader! It has already been mentioned that Elijah had a spirit that was humble, hungry for God, open and receptive, filled with faith, overflowing with the anointing of the Holy Spirit, and willing to persevere during the most difficult of circumstances. Because of Elisha's submission and servitude towards Elijah, the very same qualities that made Elijah such a tremendous man of God were imparted and developed in Elisha. The same thing had taken place in Joshua through the impartation that he received from Moses.

> *Now Joshua son of Nun was filled with the spirit of wisdom because Moses had laid his hands on him. (Deuteronomy 34:9, NIV)*

I've experienced this in my own life. It's amazing that when people see me minister they say it's like seeing my leader minister. (Although, of course, my leader ministers with greater maturity and anointing.) However, such ministry only began to flow through me when I embraced the cross of Jesus and began to submit to the leader the Lord put over me. It was then that the Lord really started using my leader's ministry to impart the life and ministry of Christ into me. In fact, the tremendous importance of what was happening in my life was revealed to me while I was sitting in a service listening to my leader preach. The Lord spoke to my heart and said, "Bone of his bones, flesh of his flesh". Up until that time I thought that scripture was only speaking about a marriage relationship. But I began to understand that the principle revealed in that scripture deals with much more than the relationship between a husband and wife. It also speaks of those who are united by calling, vision, and ministry. The Lord was telling me that He had made me a son to my leader so that I would share in his calling, vision, and ministry. I didn't realize it then, but the Lord was preparing me to start receiving the "spirit" of my leader so that the ministry I saw in him would be able to flow through me. Since that day I have never been the same, for the same demonstration of the Spirit in my leader's ministry gradually began to flow through me! That was the beginning of a new day in my life and ministry! Thank God for Christlike leaders! Nothing can take their place in helping you demonstrate the gospel of Jesus Christ!

### *Pause & Reflect*

1. Many people received ministry from Elijah, but Elisha received an impartation of Elijah's spirit (2 Kings 2:9-14). What did Elisha do that made that possible?

2. Tell how your life has been changed since you started submitting to your Christlike leader.

## Demonstrating The Gospel Reveals Jesus Christ

The purpose for signs, wonders, and miracles is for Jesus Christ to be revealed and glorified. Therefore, no matter what else is accomplished through the powerful demonstration of the gospel, the revelation of Jesus Christ is paramount. You've got to keep this in mind as you seek the Lord for miraculous ministry. Jesus warned that in the last days there will be those who have miraculous ministries, who called themselves Christians, but won't be true disciples of Jesus.

# CALLED TO DEMONSTRATE THE GOSPEL OF JESUS CHRIST

> *Not everyone who says to me, 'Lord, Lord,' will enter the kingdom of heaven, but only the one who does the will of my Father who is in heaven. Many will say to me on that day, 'Lord, Lord, did we not prophesy in your name and in your name drive out demons and in your name perform many miracles?' Then I will tell them plainly, 'I never knew you. Away from me, you evildoers!' (Matthew 7:21–23, NIV)*

In this scripture the Lord gives a key to being a true vessel of the miraculous. You must do more than call Jesus your Lord, you must have the evidence of it in your life through holy living. Jesus made it plain that miracles are not necessarily a validation of a person's relationship with God. The true test is the righteous behavior of a person as seen in his or her daily life. That's why, if you are to be a true vessel through whom Jesus can demonstrate His gospel with signs, wonders, and miracles you must also have a Christlike life! The Lord isn't looking for "showmen" who can entertain, but for disciples who will reveal Christ in their lives and ministries. Remember that Christlike ministry flows out of Christlike lives! So, when you consider what is necessary for a miraculous ministry you've got to start with the revelation of the life of Christ in you. In other words, the demonstration of the Gospel starts with a Christlike life!

Unfortunately, throughout Church history two extremes have been prevalent. There are those who emphasize a Christlike life, and others who emphasize Christlike ministry. Those who see the need for Christlike lives too often minimize the need for demonstrating the power of God through Christlike ministry. But even worse is the other extreme that emphasizes Christlike ministry with signs, wonders, and miracles with little to no emphasis on the necessity of a Christlike life. The Lord wants His disciples to represent both! Thankfully, both a godly life and powerful ministry were seen in Elisha. He not only demonstrated a godly life, but he also demonstrated the power of the Lord in his ministry. That is the reason the Lord spent such a great deal of time preparing Elisha. The Lord was going to use Elisha to perform signs, wonders, and miracles that would attract the attention of nations! If Elisha's life had not been a revelation of the life of the Lord, then his ministry would have done more harm than good, no matter how mighty the miracles were!

An example of what happens when powerful ministry is separated from a godly life is found in Balaam, an Old Testament prophet. Balaam had one of the most powerful prophetic ministries of his day and was used by the Lord to give one of the greatest Messianic prophecies of the Bible.

> *I see him, but not now; I behold him, but not near. A star will come out of Jacob; a scepter will rise out of Israel. (Numbers 24:17, NIV)*

However, after careful study you will find that Balaam had a corrupt life that lusted after power and money. In fact, it was for money that Balaam taught the Moabites what they needed to do to provoke God to judge Israel.

> *… Balaam, who taught Balak to entice the Israelites to sin so that they ate food sacrificed to idols and committed sexual immorality. (Revelation 2:14, NIV)*

Balaam's prophetic ministry was accurate, but his life was corrupt, thus his legacy is a sad commentary of what happens when a gifted disciple isn't godly!

That's why the Lord dealt with Elisha's life for so long and with such depth before he was revealed as a powerful prophet. The Lord was making sure that Elisha's life was going to be a true example of godliness. It's interesting that in all the years

# CALLED TO DEMONSTRATE THE GOSPEL OF JESUS CHRIST

Elisha served Elijah there is no mention of him being used miraculously. However, during that time Elisha was an example of the servitude of the Lord, and out of his life of servitude a miraculous ministry was born. From the very beginning of Elisha's calling the revelation of the life of the Lord was the foundation of everything he did.

Now let's look at some examples of how the life of the Lord was revealed through Elisha after he entered into the fullness of his prophetic ministry. Like Elijah, Elisha became known throughout the nations as a true prophet of the Lord. Everyone, even the ungodly, knew that when you heard from Elisha, you were hearing from the Lord!

> But Jehoshaphat asked, "Is there no prophet of the Lord here, through whom we may inquire of the Lord?" An officer of the king of Israel answered, "Elisha son of Shaphat is here. He used to pour water on the hands of Elijah." Jehoshaphat said, "The word of the Lord is with him." (2 Kings 3:11-12, NIV)

As a prophet of the Lord, Elisha was a true representative of the Lord Himself. He was a man of God through whom the life of the Lord was being revealed! It could be said of Elisha that he demonstrated the "word of the Lord" with his life. Because of this, the Lord was able to use Elisha to minister before all types of people, even Kings, knowing that Elisha wouldn't compromise his life or message. In fact, although he was respectful of authority, he didn't allow a person's position to deter him from speaking the truth! Notice how Elisha dealt respectfully, yet truthfully with Kings.

> Jehoshaphat said, "The word of the Lord is with him." So the king of Israel and Jehoshaphat and the king

> *of Edom went down to him. Elisha said to the king of Israel, "Why do you want to involve me? Go to the prophets of your father and the prophets of your mother." "No," the king of Israel answered, "because it was the Lord who called us three kings together to deliver us into the hands of Moab." Elisha said, "As surely as the Lord Almighty lives, whom I serve, if I did not have respect for the presence of Jehoshaphat king of Judah, I would not pay any attention to you. But now bring me a harpist." While the harpist was playing, the hand of the Lord came on Elisha and he said, "This is what the Lord says: ... (2 Kings 3:12–16, NIV)*

It is apparent that Elisha wouldn't compromise his life or message to impress Kings. (However, this in no way gives any disciple of the Lord the right to be disrespectful to authority. Paul dealt very strongly with that in Romans 13.) Yet, the point being made is that Elisha wouldn't compromise himself to impress anyone. In every situation and through every test Elisha desired for his life to be a true revelation of the Lord.

Not only was Elisha's life exemplary, but so was his ministry as the Lord used him to reveal His mighty power! In fact, the power of God was revealed through Elisha's ministry in many different ways.

- **The Power Of God Through Preaching And Teaching**

While there are no scriptural records of Elisha's preaching and teaching, the object lessons that the Lord gave him taught powerful truths and demonstrated the power of God!

> *The people of the city said to Elisha, "Look, our lord, this town is well situated, as you can see, but the water*

> *is bad and the land is unproductive." "Bring me a new bowl," he said, "and put salt in it." So they brought it to him. Then he went out to the spring and threw the salt into it, saying, "This is what the Lord says: 'I have healed this water. Never again will it cause death or make the land unproductive.'" And the water has remained pure to this day, according to the word Elisha had spoken. (2 Kings 2:19-22, NIV)*

This was not only a miracle, but it was a powerful object lesson full of symbolism about the life of Christ. Even Jesus used salt as a symbol of the Christlike life and ministry He would give His disciples.[1] In fact, one of the trademarks of the preaching and teaching of the disciples was that it was accompanied by the miraculous ministry of Jesus!

> *Then the disciples went out and preached everywhere, and the Lord worked with them and confirmed his word by the signs that accompanied it. (Mark 16:20, NIV)*

If you desire to have a miraculous ministry like the disciples, you should take note of what you are preaching and teaching. The scriptures reveal that Paul's miraculous ministry was always united to his message about Jesus Christ and the cross. You'd be wise to take note of this, for if your preaching and teaching aren't focused on Jesus and Him crucified, you aren't saying anything that the Lord would want to confirm with His miraculous ministry!

> *When I came to you, I did not come with eloquence or human wisdom as I proclaimed to you the testimony about God. For I resolved to know nothing while I was with you except Jesus Christ and him crucified. I came*

> *to you in weakness with great fear and trembling. My message and my preaching were not with wise and persuasive words, but with a demonstration of the Spirit's power, so that your faith might not rest on human wisdom, but on God's power. (1 Corinthians 2:1-5, NIV)*

- **The Power Of God Through Prophetic Ministry**

The power of God was revealed through Elisha's prophetic ministry. The very nature of a prophetic ministry is demonstrative. It gives birth to the manifestation of whatever the Lord has spoken through the prophet. (Prophetic ministry doesn't always bring an immediate manifestation, in fact, in most cases it doesn't. However, there was often an immediate manifestation through the prophetic ministry of Elisha.) There are numerous examples of how the Lord used Elisha's prophetic ministry to reveal the power of God. Once, Elisha prophesied concerning a city's poisonous water supply which the Lord miraculously made pure.

> *"This is what the Lord says: 'I have healed this water. Never again will it cause death or make the land unproductive.'" And the water has remained pure to this day, according to the word Elisha had spoken. (2 Kings 2:21-22, NIV)*

Another example is when Elisha prophesied that the Lord would provide water during a time of battle.

> *So the king of Israel set out with the king of Judah and the king of Edom. After a roundabout march of seven days, the army had no more water for themselves or for the animals with them. ... and he said, "This is*

> what the Lord says: I will fill this valley with pools of water. For this is what the Lord says: You will see neither wind nor rain, yet this valley will be filled with water, and you, your cattle and your other animals will drink. ... The next morning, about the time for offering the sacrifice, there it was—water flowing from the direction of Edom! And the land was filled with water. (2 Kings 3:9, 16-17, 20, NIV)

Yet another demonstration of God's power due to the prophetic ministry of Elisha was during a citywide famine. Elisha prophesied that there would be an abundance of food the very next day, which of course was accomplished just as he had said!

> Elisha replied, "Hear the word of the Lord. This is what the Lord says: About this time tomorrow, a seah of the finest flour will sell for a shekel and two seahs of barley for a shekel at the gate of Samaria." (2 Kings 7:1, NIV)

- **The Power Of God Through Healing Ministry**

The power of God was revealed through Elisha's healing ministry.

> When Elisha reached the house, there was the boy lying dead on his couch. He went in, shut the door on the two of them and prayed to the Lord. Then he got on the bed and lay on the boy, mouth to mouth, eyes to eyes, hands to hands. As he stretched himself out on him, the boy's body grew warm. Elisha turned away and walked back and forth in the room and then got on the bed and stretched out on him once more. The

> *boy sneezed seven times and opened his eyes. (2 Kings 4:32–35, NIV)*

The healing of physical bodies brings the reality of God's power into people's lives. In fact, as you read the Gospels you'll see the crowds crying out to Jesus for His healing touch more than for anything else. It seems that the Lord Jesus used healing as a door opener to get to the heart of man. It is often through the ministry of healing that people begin to understand that the Lord is real and is concerned about them.

It's awesome to realize that the Lord has given us His power and authority to heal the sick in His Name! May the Church rise up and demonstrate the Gospel to the sick and see them miraculously healed in Jesus Name!

> *And these signs will accompany those who believe: In my name ... they will place their hands on sick people, and they will get well." (Mark 16:17–18, NIV)*
>
> *It is by the name of Jesus Christ of Nazareth, whom you crucified but whom God raised from the dead, that this man stands before you healed. (Acts 4:10, NIV)*

- ### The Power Of God Through Miracles

The power of God was revealed through the miracles that Elisha performed. In fact, miracles were one of the most demonstrative aspects of Elisha's ministry. They were numerous and powerful!

> *He took the cloak that had fallen from Elijah and struck the water with it. "Where now is the Lord, the God of Elijah?" he asked. When he struck the water,*

# CALLED TO DEMONSTRATE THE GOSPEL OF JESUS CHRIST

*it divided to the right and to the left, and he crossed over. (2 Kings 2:14, NIV)*

Other miracles were the miraculous supply of oil to a widow (2 Kings 4:1-7), the removal of the poisonous contamination in the food (2 Kings 4:38-41), the food that was multiplied to feed one hundred men (2 Kings 4:42-44), and the ax head that was made to float in water for its retrieval (2 Kings 6:1-6). Each one of these miracles was a demonstrative revelation of the Lord's presence, concern, and love for His people.

People still need the miraculous intervention of the Lord today! Believe God like Elisha did and let the miraculous ministry of the Lord be revealed through you!

### Pause & Reflect

1. What is the purpose for signs, wonders, and miracles?

2. In Matthew 7:21-23 Jesus made it clear that miracles are not necessarily a validation of a person's relationship with God. How can you know whether a person with a miraculous ministry is sent from God?

3. Some people emphasize the need for a Christlike life but minimize the need for miraculous ministry. Others emphasize Christlike ministry with signs, wonders, and miracles with little to no emphasis on the necessity of a Christlike life. Why are both of these extremes damaging to the growth of God's Kingdom?

4. List several ways in which the power of God was revealed through Elisha's ministry.

## Picking Up The Mantle

The day came for Elisha to pick up the cloak of Elijah. It was time for him to see for himself that the same God who used Elijah would also use him. I believe that day has come for the Church. Those who have been hungering for more of Jesus have been crying out, "Where now is the LORD, the God of Elijah?" and I believe the Lord is answering back,

> *And surely I am with you always, to the very end of the age." (Matthew 28:20, NIV)*

You've heard the call of Jesus ... and many of you have answered His call. Now it's time to pick up His mantle and see the great things He can and will do through you!

> *They will proclaim my glory among the nations. (Isaiah 66:19, NIV)*

### Pause & Reflect

1. In what ways do you believe the Lord wants to use you to reveal His life and ministry?

2. What are you doing during this season of your life so that the life and ministry of Jesus will be revealed in and through you?

---

1. Matthew 5:13

# GET A FREE
# SPIRIT-FILLED DISCIPLESHIP NOTEBOOK

- All the "Pause & Reflect" questions from all three books in the SPIRIT-FILLED DISCIPLESHIP SERIES are conveniently put together in one notebook.

- The printable PDF version gives you plenty of space to answer each question.

- Additional room is given for you to take notes while you study privately or in a group setting.

- Just print it out and you're ready to go!

**To get it FREE go to ...**
https://subscribepage.io/Notebook

# Get The Whole Series!

## THE SPIRIT-FILLED DISCIPLESHIP SERIES

# Leave A Review On Amazon!

If you enjoyed **SPIRIT-FILLED DISCIPLESHIP: HOW GOD CALLS CHRISTLIKE DISCIPLES** please leave a review on Amazon! Your review will really make a difference and it'll only take you a moment.

https://mybook.to/Spirit-filled-Discipleship-How-God-Calls

Made in the USA
Columbia, SC
10 July 2023